YOUNG EUROPEAN GRAPHIC DESIGNERS

daab

Introduction 4

INTRODUCTION

How do you become a successful designer, relying 100% on yourself to create original work? And how do you stay original while being involved with design and with other designers constantly influencing you? The design world has changed: notwithstanding that there is now universal access to programs like Photoshop or Indesign, and that tutorials in basic principles like "rule of threes" and "white space" can be found anywhere online, there seems to have been a real shift in the way design is taught and briefs are explored in design degree courses. It used to be that there were rigorous rules to follow in order to create good work, and, correspondingly, assignments followed this approach with imposed rules to develop an understanding of the tension between structure and freedom. Now self-expression and experimentation are being pushed forward, with all the pros and cons that might transpire, and students are encouraged to broaden their approach to projects and develop an inter-disciplinary disposition. Hence an expanded perception of graphic design: you will find that many of the graphic designers featured in this book have assimilated at least one other related creative practice to their field, be it illustration, photography, art direction or typography. Thanks to a thriving style and culture industry coupled with a unique art and design- school environment, European capitals from Amsterdam to Zagreb are currently a hotbed of small eclectic graphic studios and teams of designers. There is a desire to create independent practices and an aspiration to cross borders, all the while retaining a specific national flavour. Locality and the value of cultural background are explored, but not exploited. Influences are equally inspired by European vanguard movements, American commerce, contemporary pop culture and the blazing trail marked by prolific studios like Graphic Thought Facility, Base or Non Format –multi-cultural practices which have achieved huge commercial success and yet have remained adventurous and experimental. Artistry and craft seem to have made a triumphant comeback to the front line, and are being redefined for the next generation. Young Europeans are in a promising position, and if the level of quality work and quality clients is maintained, there is much to look forward to in the years to come.

Wie wird man ein erfolgreicher Designer, der sich selbst und seiner Originalität hundertprozentig vertraut? Und wie bleibt man originell, ungeachtet des beständigen Einflusses anderer Designer? Die Welt des Designs hat sich verändert – nicht nur durch Programme wie Photoshop und Indesign oder durch Online-Tutorien mit Anleitungen zu Themen wie Goldener Schnitt oder Weißraum. In der Art, wie Design unterrichtet und wie Konzepte entwickelt werden, hat sich offenbar ein echter Wandel vollzogen. Früher gab es strikte Regeln für die Entwicklung einer qualitativ hochwertigen Gestaltung. Bei der Aufgabenstellung galten strenge Vorgaben, die ein spannungsreiches Verhältnis zwischen gestalterischer Freiheit und Struktur bewirkten. Heute werden eher persönliche Ausdrucksstärke und Experimentierfreude erwartet - mit allen sich daraus ergebenden, manchmal auch widersprüchlichen Konsequenzen. Studenten werden ermutigt, ihren Projektansatz auszubauen und zusätzlich interdisziplinäre Fähigkeiten zu erwerben. Die Folge ist eine breiter gefächerte gestalterische Wahrnehmung. Das zeigt sich auch bei den Graphikdesignern, die in diesem Buch vorgestellt werden. Viele haben eine zusätzliche, kreative Disziplin in ihren Schaffensprozess einbezogen, sei es Illustration, Fotografie, Kunst oder Typografie. Die europäischen Hauptstädte von Amsterdam bis Zagreb sind derzeit florierende Geburtsstätten für kleine, vielseitige Graphikstudios und Designerteams. Die kulturelle Vielfalt und sehr unterschiedliche Stilrichtungen ermöglichen die Entwicklung von Originalität und schaffen ein einzigartiges Umfeld, auch für Kunst- und Designunterricht. Überall zeigt sich unabhängiges, grenzüberschreitendes Schaffen, oft jedoch unter Wahrung eines nationalen Geschmacks. Kulturelle Hintergründe werden zwar erkundet, aber nicht immer verarbeitet. Inspirationen erhalten die jungen Designer von der europäischen Avantgarde, vom amerikanischen Kommerzdenken wie auch von der zeitgenössischen Popkultur. Trendsetter sind originelle Studios wie Graphic Thought Facility, Base oder Non Format, - multi-kulturelle Büros, die riesigen kommerziellen Erfolg erzielt haben und dennoch wagemutig und experimentell geblieben sind. Ein triumphales Comeback haben Kunst und Handwerk. Sie werden derzeit neu definiert. Junge Europäer sind in einer viel versprechenden Position. Sofern das Qualitätsniveau des Schaffens und der Kunden gewahrt wird, gibt es viel Grund für Vorfreude auf die kommenden Jahre.

¿Cómo se convierte uno en un diseñador de éxito, confiando al 100% en sí mismo para crear una obra original? Y ¿cómo puede seguir siendo original mientras está implicado en el diseño y bajo la influencia de otros diseñadores? El mundo del diseño ya no es el mismo. Más allá de que hoy todo el mundo pueda acceder a programas como Photoshop o Indesign, y encontrar en cualquier rincón de la web cursos sobre principios básicos como la «regla de tres» o el uso de los blancos, parece haberse producido un verdadero cambio en el método de enseñanza y el enfoque propios de las licenciaturas de diseño. Hasta hace poco, para crear una obra de calidad debían respetarse reglas rigurosas y, por consecuencia, los trabajos se realizaban según normas establecidas para alcanzar un mayor conocimiento de la relación entre estructura y libertad. Actualmente, se impulsan más la expresión personal y la experimentación –con todos los pros y contras que esto comporta– y los estudiantes son animados a desarrollar su enfoque hacia las tareas y una actitud interdisciplinaria. De ahí una visión ampliada del diseño gráfico, que queda reflejada en la obra de los diseñadores gráficos que aparecen en este libro. Muchos de ellos han asimilado al menos otra práctica creativa relacionada a su campo, ya sea la ilustración, la fotografía, la dirección de arte o la tipografía. Gracias al desarrollo de los sectores de la moda y la cultura, en combinación con un ámbito de escuelas de arte y diseño único, las capitales europeas –desde Ámsterdam hasta Zagreb– se han convertido en semilleros de eclécticos estudios gráficos y equipos de diseñadores. Existe el deseo de realizar prácticas independientes y una aspiración a cruzar las fronteras, conservando a su vez cierto regusto nacional. Se exploran el sentido de la localidad y el valor de los antecedentes culturales, aunque sin explotarlos. La influencia procede tanto de los movimientos europeos de vanguardia, de la industria estadounidense y de la cultura pop contemporánea como del camino marcado por estudios prolíficos como Graphic Thought Facility, Base o Non Format –prácticas multiculturales que han alcanzado un éxito comercial aplastante, conservando su línea aventurera y experimental–. El arte y la artesanía han vuelto a ocupar un posición de primer plano y se están redefiniendo para las próximas generaciones. Los jóvenes europeos se encuentran en una posición prometedora y, si se mantiene el nivel actual de calidad de la obra y de los clientes, todavía cabe esperar mucho más en los próximos años.

Comment devient-on un designer à succès, en comptant à 100% sur soi pour créer des travaux originaux? Comment rester original malgré le travail des autres designers qui vous influence en permanence? Le monde du design a changé –sans parler de la facilité d'accès à des programmes tels que Photoshop ou Indesign, ou les formations aux principes de base du type «règle des tiers» et «espace blanc», disponibles à tous les coins du Web– l'enseignement du design et l'analyse des descriptifs ont subi un réel changement dans les formations diplômantes. Il fut un temps où un bon travail passait par des règles strictes, et, parallèlement, les commandes respectaient ce principe de règles imposées pour développer la compréhension de la tension entre structure et liberté. Aujourd'hui, avec ses avantages et ses inconvénients, l'expression individuelle et l'expérimentation sont mises en avant et l'on pousse les étudiants à élargir leur approche des projets et à développer un état d'esprit interdisciplinaire. Il en découle une perception diversifiée du design; vous noterez que plusieurs des designers inclus dans ce livre ont incorporé au moins une autre pratique créative dans leur travail, que ce soit l'illustration, la photographie, la création artistique ou la typographie. Grâce à des industries florissantes du style et de la culture, combinées à un environnement unique au niveau de l'enseignement artistique, les capitales européennes, sont des viviers de petits studios graphique et d'équipes de designers éclectiques. Le désir de créer des unités indépendantes, enracinées dans leur terreau national mais cependant trans-frontalières, est partout présent. Les valeurs locales et le passé culturel sont explorés, mais sans abus. L'avant-garde européenne, le commerce US, la pop culture contemporaine et l'exemple de studios prolifiques et multiculturels comme Graphic Thought Facility, Base ou Non Format qui, malgré leur immense succès commercial, sont restés aussi audacieux qu'expérimentaux, influent à part égale. Le talent et la patte de l'artiste font un retour triomphant au premier plan, et sont redéfinis pour la prochaine génération. Les jeunes européens sont en position favorable, et si la qualité du travail et des clients est maintenue, l'avenir se présente sous les meilleurs auspices.

Come si può diventare un disegnatore grafico di successo facendo affidamento su sé stessi al 100% per creare opere originali? Come riuscire a differenziarsi dal resto pur rimanendo a stretto contatto con il mondo del disegno ed esposti all'influenza di altri grafici? Il mondo del disegno è cambiato: al di là del fatto che programmi come Photoshop o Indesign sono oggi alla portata di tutti, e che tutoriali su principi basici come la «regola dei terzi» e lo spazio bianco si trovano ovunque su Internet, sembra che qualcosa sia cambiato davvero nel modo d'insegnare e d'intendere i progetti di disegno grafico nelle università. In passato si affermava la necessità di attenersi a regole rigorose per realizzare buone creazioni, di conseguenza le esercitazioni si basavano su principi imposti con l'obiettivo di comprendere la tensione tra struttura e libertà. Oggi si privilegia l'espressione individuale e la sperimentazione, con tutti i pro e i contro che ciò comporta, mentre gli studenti sono spinti ad avere un approccio più amplio ai progetti e a svilupparne il carattere interdisciplinare. Ne deriva un concetto allargato di disegno grafico, rispecchiato dal contenuto di questo libro. Molti dei designer che compaiono qui praticano almeno un'altra disciplina creativa collegata al proprio campo: illustrazione, fotografia, direzione artistica o tipografia. Grazie al buon momento attraversato dall'industria della cultura e della moda, così come all'ambiente unico che si respira in molte scuole d'arte e design, le capitali europee, da Amsterdam a Zagabria, sono oggi terreno fertile per piccoli ed eclettici studi e team grafici accomunati dal desiderio di creare pratiche indipendenti e superare frontiere, pur mantenendo un certo carattere nazionale. La tradizione e la cultura locali sono esplorate ma non saccheggiate, e le influenze possono provenire sia dalle avanguardie europee, dall'industria americana e dalla cultura pop contemporanea sia dalle nuove strade aperte da studi prolifici come Graphic Thought Facility, Base o Non Format. Questi ultimi hanno affermato pratiche multiculturali capaci di raggiungere uno straordinario successo commerciale pur mantenendosi audaci e sperimentali. L'arte e l'artigianato sembrano essere tornati alla ribalta e sono reinterpretati ad uso delle generazioni future. I giovani europei hanno molto da offrire e, se si mantiene l'attuale livello di qualità delle opere e dei clienti, ci si può aspettare molto di più per il futuro.

**ALL THE WAY TO PARIS | COPENHAGEN, DENMARK/
MALMÖ, SWEDEN**
Tanja Vibe, Petra Olsson Glendt, Cecilie Svanberg

Partners Tanja Vibe, Petra Olsson Gendt and Cecilie Svanberg founded All The Way To Paris in 2005. Educated at
the Danish School of Design in Copenhagen as well as design schools in New York, London and Paris, they operate
from offices in Copenhagen and Malmö, working on a broad
spectrum of award-winning graphic design projects.

www.allthewaytoparis.com

1 Logo and cards | Teik, 2007
2 Magazine design and art direction | Venue magazine,
  2004/05
3 Look book and identity | Eksempel, 2006/07
4 Hjem igen artbook | Mikael Andersen Gallery, 2004
5 Contributions to art fanzine | GAS, 2006/07
  Curators: Pernille Albrectsen and Jacob Fabricious
6 Visual identity | Teik, 2007
7 Visual identity | Ystad Studio, 2004

ATWT *paris*®
all the way to paris

Hermann JOSE ROSSACH
Pour, que a l'ombre natroi, crème de la crème

Planche n° 6

art Sanchez Alfonso Abbott's team
supervision Dau Ti, Andy Cabor
édition auteur forgotten media — verso Arte craft Alfonso Abbott's team
illustration Mabaste Meri, David abnist
ce o si Arte Fil
auteur Santa Leti abdco

Planche n° 7

EKSEMPEL

EKSEMPEL AUTUMN/WINTER 2007

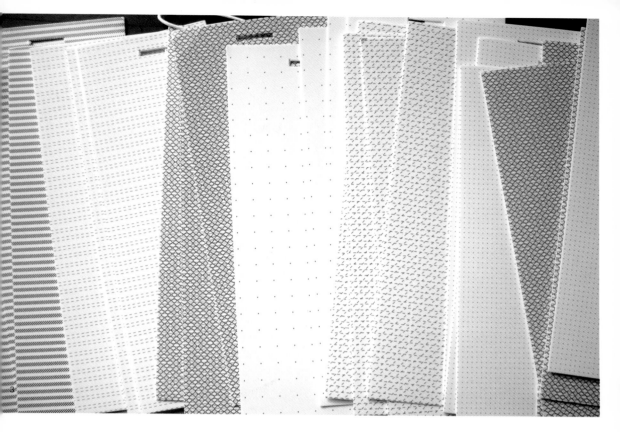

TRESVERDIGES BORD, DENNE TYNDE HINDE SOM ADSKILLER OG FORENER OS /
TABLE OF THICKNESS, THIS THIN MEMBRANE WHICH SEPARATES AND UNITES US 2011

GODNAT HISTORI ER/BED TIME ST ORIES

This issue of GAS is about money – which is exactly why we don't want yours. GAS 002 is free. This is not *how* to spend it (the title of the *Financial Times* lifestyle supplement). It is a fanzine written and performed by a number of writers, artists, designers and non-future educationalist, who all contributed for free. Rather, nobody is urging anybody to buy anything. But we would still like you to think about it; money, that is. We would like you to think about the journey – the stressful, troublesome or perhaps even cheerful trip – it has been on, travelling from the bazaar in Cairo to Wal-Mart, from the reverse vending machine to The Ritz. Or how it lies dormant in many different places, in messy rabbit fur handbags next to lipsticks and sweets whose wrappings have been discarded, in ashtrays, beds, muffins, kitchen cabinets or in pockets next to the crotch (face it – even money in a Good money clip still sits in the pocket close to the inner thigh). Money is dirty in many ways, and besides which, it's the most boring subject to talk about – it needs a smack in the eye. As the Danish bard Dan Turèll once said: *"Penge er dønenes farlige"* (Money is deadly dangerous).

Apart from our faithful GAS correspondents – Peio Aguirre (Donostia-San Sebastián...

La Vasijio Balto (Christiansted, St. Croix), Stephan (Dülamuth (Munich), Theresa L. Duncan (Los Angeles), Matías Faldbakken (Oslo), Lars Erik Frank (Copenhagen), Karl Holmqvist (Stockholm/Berlin), Nontsikelelo 'Lolo' Veleko (Johannesburg), and YOUNG-HAE CHANG HEAVY INDUSTRIES (Seoul) – we are pleased to introduce our guest contributors, Lucy R. Lippard (Galisteo Basin), Meta Haven (Amsterdam), Anna Maria Helgadóttir (Copenhagen), Toke Lykkeberg Nielsen (Copenhagen), and Dóra Nissen (Christiania).

They have all thought about it, money that is.

We are proud to be putting out another state-funded issue of GAS.

Pernille Albrethsen and Jacob Fabricius, Copenhagen.

GAS

2007 ★ 002/The Money Issue ★★★
04/05/06/50/06

"Cocaine Kate" And The Measure Of A Woman's Worth
By Theresa L. Duncan, Los Angeles

Kate Moss was recently photographed by the British director Mike Figgis for the Agent Provocateur lingerie catalog, whereafter he trilled in some nerve-jangling mania to a friend that she is "truly a supermodel, the best of the best."

Gastroville
By Peio Aguirre, Donostia-San Sebastián

San Sebastián has more Michelin stars per inhabitant than any other place on earth. Sixteen, to be precise.

teik

guldsmed   birkegade 9, st
sophie teik hansen dk- 2200 copenhagen n
                   +45 2633 5573

                   www.teik-guldsmed.dk

                   dato

arrrghh

3 COLOUR MONSTER

1

ANDY SMITH | HASTINGS, UK
Andy Smith

Andy Smith studied illustration at the Royal College of Art in London. His work combines modern technology with print techniques and drawing, resulting in digital work that has its roots in silkscreen printing. Besides commercial work he also produces self-published books, which allow him to develop his stories and characters.

www.asmithillustration.com

1 Trading card illustration | Peskimo, 2006
2 Book spreads | Self-initiated project, 2006
3 Promotional poster | Self-initiated, 2005
4 Promotional poster | Olswang, 2005
5 Illustration | Self-initiated, 2004

FATTYS HOUSE &

Lightning Strikes At

THE BIG DROP

2 NEW BOOKS By Andy Smith

the big dr@p

Lightning strikes at

FATTYS HOUSE

A lively IMAGINATION can take you ANYWHERE

4

euritmie ensemble nederland

euritmie ensemble nederland

sturm

Langsam wie ein Planet
nach einer Erzählung von Michael Ende

Sturmsonate opus 31 nr 2
Ludwig van Beethoven

Prospero
aus 'Der Sturm' von William Shakespeare

een.
euritmie ensemble nederland

DESIGN BY WWW.ANOTHERCOMPANY.ORG

ANOTHER COMPANY | UTRECHT, AMSTERDAM, THE NETHERLANDS
Joachim Baan

Joachim Baan started his career as a web and graphic designer with Internet agency Netlinq Framfab and at Oktober in Amsterdam. After a 3 year stint at Staat working on projects for Nike, Levi's and Heineken, he decided to start working as a freelance senior graphic designer and photographer under the name Another Company.

www.anothercompany.org

1 Poster | Euritmie Ensamble Nederland, 2007
2 Photography book | Self-initiated project, 2007
3 Illustration | Witte de With, 2007
4 Brochure | Baron network, 2006
  In collaboration with staat
5 Illustration for glass divider | Netherlands National Institute for Public Health and the Environment, 2007

FOR AS LONG
AS I CAN'T REMEMBER

Joachim Baan

A SOCIAL SPACE

ANOTHERCOMPANY
FOR
WITTE DE WITH

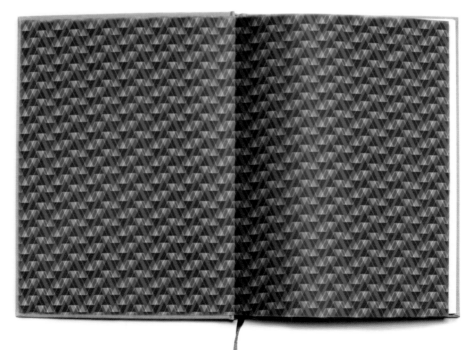

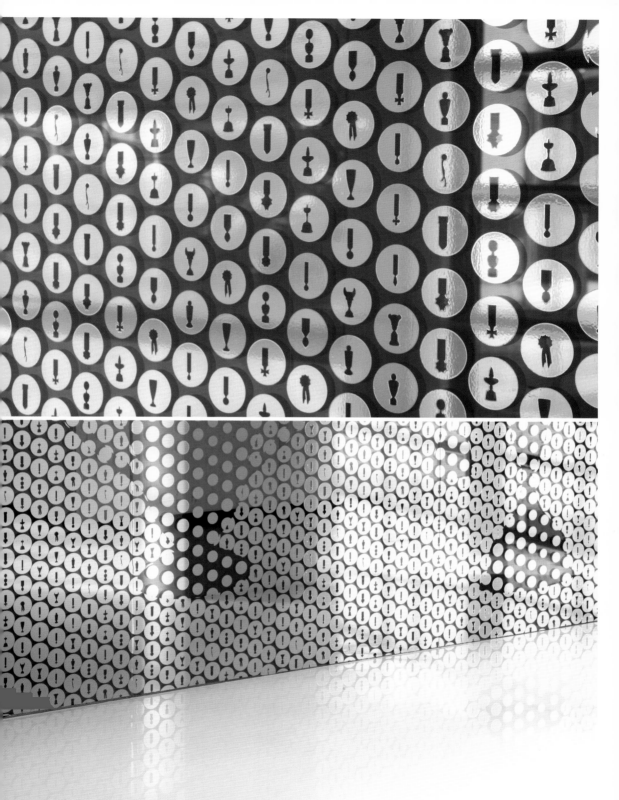

APFEL ZET | BERLIN, GERMANY

Matthias Ernstberger, Roman Bittner, Jarek Sierpinski

Matthias Ernstberger and Roman Bittner started designing together in 1996 and from 1997 onwards worked under the name Apfel Zet, later to be joined by Jarek Sierpinski in 2001. Alongside their design ventures, Apfel Zet also engage with design and architecture on a theoretical level, publishing articles on the topic across a diverse range of media.

www.apfelzet.de

1   Illustration | Illustrative Berlin 06, 2006
2   Fluke poster, tickets and postcards | Armin Beber, 2006
3   Promotional poster | Technikmuseum Berlin, 2006
4   Promotional poster | Self-initiated, 2004
5   Call Me Istanbul logo | ZKM Karlsruhe, 2004
6   Cover illustration | ProAgro Brandenburg, 2005
7   Magazine spreads | Plotki Magazine, 2006
8   Promotional poster | Lisa Bassenge and Adelheid Kleineidam, 2005
9   Logos, Ahoi-marie.com, Audiac, Ciees, Preslisa, Pyramide Bookshop | St. Moritz Automobile Club, 2004/06
10 Postcard series and promotional poster | Technikmuseum Berlin, 2006

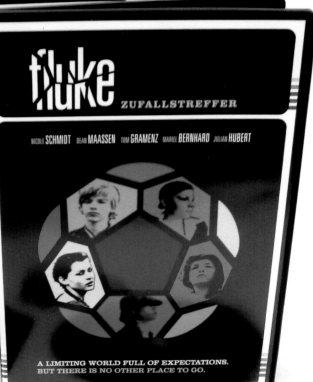

fluke
ZUFALLSTREFFER

NICOLE SCHMIDT   DEAN MAASSEN   TOM GRAMENZ   MARIEL BERNHARD   JULIAN HUBERT

A LIMITING WORLD FULL OF EXPECTATIONS.
BUT THERE IS NO OTHER PLACE TO GO.

C.U.T. Entertainme
first short film pro
had no prior invol
them the opportu
partake in the di
together they dev
were able to affor
their school, and
With a concrete pl
passion, filming b
things. Filmmakin

When
chang
in FL
lives
facing
desp
sudd

Language   German
Subtitles   English
Length   26.35 minutes
Codec   Region 0 (PAL)

KINDER ZUM OLYMP
CATEGORY FILM/NEW MEDIA
WINNER 1ST PRIS

SPECIAL FEATURES
AUDIO COMMENTARY BY DIRECTOR
MARTIN LEVIS AND PRODUCTION
MANAGER IRINA SCHWARZ

BEHIND THE SCENE:
STORYBOARD COMP
STILLS GALLERY

Coming soon...

fluke
ZUFALLSTREFFER

A LIMITING WORLD FULL OF EXPECTATIONS.
BUT THERE IS NO OTHER PLACE TO GO.

ZUFALLS fluke TREFFER

26.35 MIN (RUNNING TIME)

DIRECTED BY MARTIN LEVIS
A C.U.T. ENTERTAINMENT PRODUCTION
IN ASSOCIATION WITH THE OTHER GUY
AND ASYLUM PRODUCTIONS CORK

VEMBER 2006
IL 2007

TSCHES
HNIKMUSEUM
LIN (DTMB)
BINER STR. 9
63 BERLIN
O@DTMB.DE
W.DTMB.DE

NUNGSZEITEN :
ISTAG BIS FREITAG:
BIS 17.30 UHR
STAG/SONNTAG:
0 - 18.00 UHR
NTAGS
CHLOSSEN

ALFRED GRENANDER
ARCHTEKT DER BERLINER U-BAHN

3

FIRMEN ARCHITEKTEN
MARTIN-GROPIUS-BAU
17.4 - 22.6.2002
PETER BEHRENS · ALFRED GRENANDER
HANS HEINRICH MÜLLER · EUGEN SCHMOHL
HANS HERTLEIN · RICHARD BRADEMANN
EINE AUSSTELLUNG ZUR INDUSTRIEGESCHICHTE DER STADT BERLIN
STRESEMANNSTRASSE 110 · 10117 BERLIN · ÖFFNUNGSZEITEN: TÄGLICH 10-19 UHR · FR. 10-22 UHR

4

APRIL BIS
AUGUST 2004

E AUSSTELLUNG
RAHMEN DER
UROPÄISCHEN
URTAGE
RLSRUHE 2004

ZKM | ZENTRUM
FÜR KUNST UND
MEDIENTECHNOLOGIE
KARLSRUHE
LORENZSTRASSE 19
D-76135 KARLSRUHE
TEL.: +49 (0)721-81 00 12 00
WWW.ZKM.DE

ÖFFNUNGSZEITEN
MI. - FR. 10 - 18 UHR
SA. U. SO. 11 - 18 UHR
MO. U. DI. GESCHLOSSEN

6

L'VIV TRAIN STATION

01.25 – 06.15

Felix of Ekenstam
Stockholm

Photos:
Achim Hatzius

Spending a night in a world made of marble. With hidden entertainment behind the toilet. Surrounded by 19 year old police officers. Trying to stay awake to observe what the sleepers don't see.

01.25

We pay three hryvnia to the man behind the counter, he humbly lets us enter the VIP waiting room. People are trying to sleep on hard, but exclusive benches. A eurostyle cafeteria is selling beer and sandwiches, everything around us is made of marble.

01.34

We make our camp at one of the benches, observing the surroundings. The night guard tells us to take our bags off the bench and put it on the floor.

01.43

The hidden loudspeakers wake up and a Ukrainian medley of old eurodisco songs start echoing from the marble walls. An effective method to keep anyone from falling asleep while waiting.

02.00

A man with two golden teeth is curiously observing our digital camera.

- Is that a TV?
- No, it is a camera.

02.03

The same man asks if he can borrow it to show it to his wife.

- Of course.

They take a look. We ask if we can take a photo of them. It's not possible, it's against their religion.

02.07

Everyone who has managed despite the music to fall asleep is now effectively woken up by a man in a blue suit who is rigourously cleaning the marble floor with a huge yellow Kärcher machine.

02.45

We take a walk around the station, behind the toilet we stumble upon a shooting gallery. This seems to be the official meeting spot for some of the thirty police officers guarding the station. The chief of police

Internationalized VILLAGE

THREE EPISODES FROM AN UKRAINIAN VILLAGE

Marek Ćавíček
Praha
Eva Kvасníková
Liberec
Myroslava Kavylh
L'viv

Photos:
Jan Zappner

I.

The cigarettes and alcohol sumggled across the Ukrainian-Polish border and the sweat of Ukrainian gastarbeiters or "zarobitchany" have been transformed into bricks and cement. New houses have been built and old ones rebuilt in the village of L. in Western Ukraine.

The building standard in the village used to be a basement timbered house accompanied by a shed hosting a cow and a dry toilet. The majority of the houses still look like that. As the houses were low they used to blend into the landscape with the exceptions of the two churches and the lonely high-rise building from the Soviet era. Today the "skyline" is changing. The competition for the most visible house in the village is fierce.

Myroslav has worked in a sugar factory in the Czech Republic for five years. Together with his wife Maria he is building a new, big house in L. Their lot has changed into a construction site. They still live in the old house which is marginal in size when compared to the contours of the new one.

Maria and Myroslav represent the new housing style. Like the other high houses of "zarobitchany" their new home cannot be overlooked. When having visitors Myroslav usually brings them up the second floor. "Two floors are enough. You see everything", he says, satisfied with the view. "Here's the part of the village in the valley and on the other side there's the school and the building of the local council".

The number of floors, the decoration and appliances correspond to the steady income from abroad. The construction sites are thus projects with an open future. This depends not only on the financial resources. The final house is a mixture of new cultural influences acquired during work abroad and the wishes of the family members. Open spaces, a big kitchen for his wife Maria, a balcony, a modern bathroom including the toilet – the house owner claims to have built it in the "Czech style".

Such a life time achievement requires perfection. For example, the arrangement of the garage has been contemplated for a long time. "We decided to destroy our old garage and to construct a separate one. If it

ICH SUCHE DEINE STERNE

GEREIMTES & UNGEREIMTES · LYRIK & LOVESONGS

und WILL NICHT SCHLAFEN

GELESEN VON
Adelheid Kleineidam
GESUNGEN VON
Lisa Bassenge

DRUMS :   RALF KÜNDGEN
BASS :   PAUL KLEBER
GITARRE: JO GEHLMANN
TROMPETE: CHRISTIAN MEYERS
PIANO: SEYYIT EL CHERBINY

FREILICHTBÜHNE
AN DER ZITADELLE
SPANDAU
8

SAMSTAG, 13.08.
AM JULIUSTURM
X33, U7 ZITADELLE

BEGINN: 20:00 UHR
EINLASS: EINE STUNDE VORHER
RESERVIERUNG:030/333 40 22
TICKETS ONLINE: WWW.FREILICHTBUEHNE-SPANDAU.DE

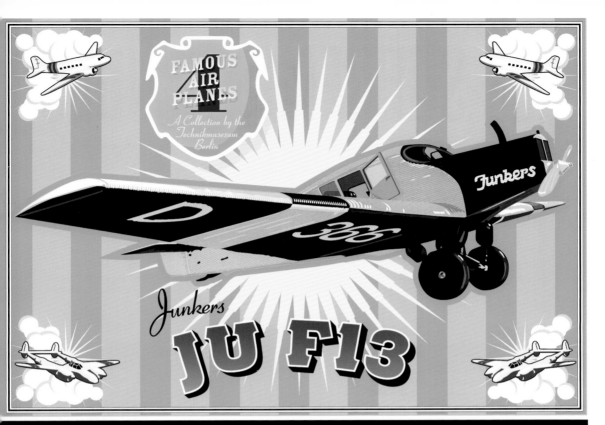

FAMOUS AIR PLANES 4

A Collection by the Technikmuseum Berlin

Junkers

JU F13

CITY·OF·NEW·YORK DEPT OF DOCKS
FLOYD · BENNETT · FIELD

LANDUNG DER FW 200 CONDOR IN NEW YORK AM 11.8.1938 NACH NORDATLANTIKFLUG

FOCKE WULF CONDOR

DER BEREICH LUFTFAHRT IM TECHNIKMUSEUM BERLIN

LES SUPREMES DINDES

Supremesdindes.com   *en Concert*

2D TOUR (SUD) • FABRICE COPELLI • 04 75 25 59 20 • 06 08 46 73 66 • FABRICE@2DTOUR.COM
2D TOUR (NORD) • ISABELLE SIRE • 03 88 28 15 18 • 06 10 83 22 11 • ISABELLE@2DTOUR.COM
CONTACT PRESSE • KAROLINE VONFELT • 06 07 16 90 39 • KAROLINE@SDV.FR

1

ARNAUD JARSAILLON | CREST, FRANCE
Arnaud Jarsaillon

After an initial career revolving around theatre, music and the arts as a decorator, musician and co-founder of Pachyderm Kréation, a collective specialized in scenography, Arnaud Jarsaillon established himself as a graphic designer in 1999, favouring a client base exclusively oriented towards the scenic arts. He lives and works in Crest, France.

www.arnaudjarsaillon.net

1 Concert poster | 2Dtour and Wagram, 2005
2 Danse au fil d'avril festival poster | Fédération des oeuvres laïques, 2007
3 La Désaccordée poster | Théâtre de Cornouaille, 2006
4 Le livre au vert festival poster | Parc Natural Régional du Pilat, 2002
5 Promotional poster | Comédie de Valence, 2005
6 Alba la Romaine festival posters | Comédie de Valence, 2006/07

LES FÉDÉRATIONS DES ŒUVRES LAÏQUES DE LA DRÔME ET DE L'ARDÈCHE PRÉSENTENT

DANSE
AU FIL D'AVRIL
DU 13 AVRIL AU 06 MAI 2007
DRÔME _ ARDÈCHE
SPECTACLES - RENCONTRES - STAGES
FOL26. 0475824479 FOL07. 0475202701 FOL07.COM

SEIZIÈME ÉDITION

16

3

la
désaccordée

SAISON 2005 · 2006

Comédie
de Valence
centre dramatique national
drôme — ardèche

INFORMATIONS / RÉSERVATIONS 04 75 78 41 70   WWW.COMEDIEDEVALENCE.COM

FESTIVAL ORGANISÉ PAR LA COMÉDIE DE VALENCE COM DA.

FESTIVAL D'ALBA LA ROMAINE
ARDÈCHE
15-27 JUILLET 06

"LES PASSIONS"
+
"A LA SCÈNE DES ARTISANS"
+
"SANS TITRE"
MIS EN SCÈNE
JEAN-YVES MACHON
AVEC LES COMÉDIENS
DE LA TROUPE PERMANENTE
DE LA COMÉDIE DE VALENCE

**DARIO FO
SHAKESPEARE
GARCIA LORCA
SÉNÈQUE**

"LES TROYENNES"
PAR LA SCÈNE
CAROLINE MARCADÉ
DU 15 AU 27 JUILLET 06

BUREAU DU FESTIVAL 04 75 52 45 81   VENTE EN LIGNE WWW.COMEDIEDEVALENCE.COM

FESTIVAL EST ORGANISÉ PAR LA COMÉDIE DE VALENCE, CDN DRÔME ARDÈCHE, SUBVENTIONNÉ PAR LE CONSEIL GÉNÉRAL DE L'ARDÈCHE LE CONSEIL RÉGIONAL RHÔNE-ALPES. AVEC LE SOUTIEN DE LA MAIRIE D'ALBA, ALBA, EN PARTENARIAT AVEC L'ASSOCIATION ENFANTS ET AMIS D'ALBA, LE SITE ARCHÉOLOGIQUE D'ALBA LA ROMAINE

Terre d'Ardèche   RhôneAlpes   Mairie d'Alba

FESTIVAL D'ALBA LA ROMAINE
ARDÈCHE
13 → 26 JUILLET 2007

DOM JUAN
THÉÂTRE
MOLIÈRE / YAN-JOËL COLLIN
DOM 15, SAM 14, DIM 15
MAR 18, MER 28, JEU 19
VEN 20, SAM 21 JUILLET 2007
AVEC LES COMÉDIENS PERMANENTS
DE LA COMÉDIE DE VALENCE

LES VISIONNAIRES
THÉÂTRE
DESMARETS DE SAINT-SORLIN /
CHRISTIAN SCHIARETTI
AVEC LES ÉLÈVES DE LA 65ᵉ PROMOTION
DE L'ENSATT
MAR 24, MER 25,
JEU 26 JUILLET 2007

BUREAU DU FESTIVAL 04 75 52 45 81   VENTE EN LIGNE WWW.COMEDIEDEVALENCE.COM

FESTIVAL EST ORGANISÉ PAR LA COMÉDIE DE VALENCE, CDN DRÔME ARDÈCHE, SUBVENTIONNÉ PAR LE CONSEIL GÉNÉRAL DE L'ARDÈCHE LE CONSEIL RÉGIONAL RHÔNE-ALPES. AVEC LE SOUTIEN DE LA MAIRIE D'ALBA, ALBA, EN PARTENARIAT AVEC L'ASSOCIATION ENFANTS ET AMIS D'ALBA, LE SITE ARCHÉOLOGIQUE D'ALBA LA ROMAINE

Terre d'Ardèche   RhôneAlpes   Mairie d'Alba

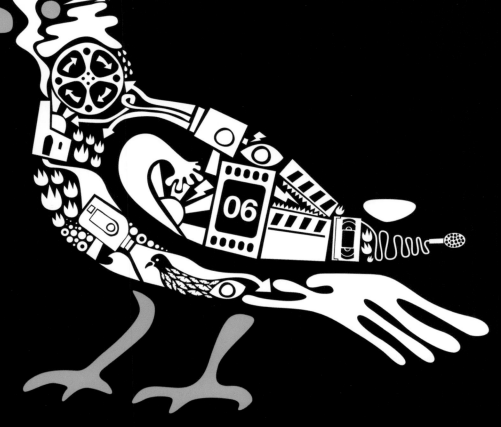

A-SIDE | FALMOUTH, UK
Alex Rowse, Ross Imms

A-Side is a graphic design and illustration studio based in Cornwall. Working on everything from advertisements and websites to t-shirts and posters, as well as taking care of art direction duties at Stranger and September magazines, A-Side are constantly generating new ideas, working late, playing lots and keeping their minds lucid.

www.a-sidestudio.co.uk

1 Promotional flyer and poster | Cornwall Film Festival, 2006
2 Assorted magazine spreads | Stranger Publications, 2005/07
3 Catalogue | Cornish Oasis, 2007
   Illustration by Jenny Bowers
4 Rairbirds 1 CD packaging | One Little Indian records, 2007
5 Promotional flyer | Jam records, 2007
6 Promotional catalogue | Loose-Fit surf shop, 2006

AARON ROSE AND ALLEGED GALLERY 1992-2002

words: *Aaron Rose*

"I never wanted to be an art dealer. I didn't have any art world experience. I just had a space and so we started putting up shows and we called the gallery Alleged after these (alleged) good luck candies that they sold in the Puerto Rican grocery stores. It was an Alleged gallery, not really a gallery."
~ *Aaron Rose*

"The gallery was most known for dealing with artists coming out of skateboarding. I worked very closely with Mark Gonzales, Barry McGee, Mike Mills, Ed Templeton - skateboarding, graffiti, street culture stuff."
~ *Aaron Rose*

"For years and years we were just ignored by the high establishment. But I think that is more their problem than a problem with the art...This kind of art, it's like the new American folk art. Much like in the way jazz and blues was."
~ *Aaron Rose*

This is Chris Johanson building a massive installation of traffic, buildings and hot-air balloons when we went to Tokyo together in 2001. The whole thing was built out of cardboard, wood and duct-tape. *Photo: Ivory Serra*

STRANGER SOUNDS SPECIAL

illustration: jenny bowers www.jennybowers.co.uk

'Beginnings' in music is an evasive subject; full of debate and opinion weaved together with myths and downright lies. Who and what were the firsts in any given era or genre is almost impossible to pin down. So what follows is a loose appraisal of the term as Stranger takes a look at some originators, pioneers and upstarts.

First, a word on format...

The history of the vinyl record is nothing if not convoluted. Ten-inch discs of shellac resin were quick to replace Thomas Edison's clunky cylinder-based recording system. The discovery of vinyl in the 1920s saw Columbia introduce double sided discs for the first time, eventually replacing the easily broken and short capacity of the 78 rpm shellac discs with a 33 rpm 12" disc in the late 1940s.

RCA soon gazumped the company, taking advantage of the much quieter surfaces of the new material to introduce their 7" micro groove, which became the standard format for the stackable jukebox in the 1950s. Its 45 rpm rotation was the first to be determined by calculus – sonic scientists having determined that a constant rotational speed occurred when the innermost recorded diameter measured half the outermost recorded diameter – hence the three-inch diameter label on 7" singles.

The 12" single arrived by way of disco. Longer dance mixes were initially issued to DJs as 12" test pressings as early as the first half of the 1970s as the wider grooves of the larger record allowed for a better sound quality. It took five years before labels such as Stax, Wand and Salsoul began to supply record shops with these limited editions, and they soon became the club DJ's weapon of choice in the second half of the 1970s.

The digital era began in 1982, with the arrival of the compact disc. Sony and Phillips had been working on developing a new format for some years, with the electrickery of sampling rates, encoding conventions and file storage nailed down in a technical manual known as the Red Book. With digital music players and the massive storage of next century formats such as Sony's Blu-Ray enabling us to float free of any physical record collections, collecting vinyl has become something of a resistance movement.

But what is so attractive about the humble record? As Melodic's David Cooper puts it, "you can feel the weight of vinyl in your hands, see the grooves and physically put the needle on the record and, in doing so, you make a tangible connection." +
Kingsley Marshall

SURF

words by
Dan Crockett

photography by
John Eldridge

RHYTHM OF THE TIDES

KERNOW HAS ALWAYS BEEN AT THE MERCY OF THE TIDES, BUT FOR THE DILIGENT, THERE ARE TREASURES TO BE FOUND.

The moon turns the tides gently away and before the sun sneaks out of the East, boards are laying on the frosty ground. The suits frozen with yesterday's sand and piss are already halfway on: late winter on the South Coast and an empty dawn patrol. Breath condenses in the air. Up and down the coast, beaches that will be firing in three hours are flooded over and above the usual high tide mark. A spring high tide is holding the swell down, yet one particular reef is perfection. Groomed lefts peel over submerged rock as dawn breaks. Within a few hours, as the rest of the coast comes into its own and the roads begin to buzz with cars, this same spot will waver and pinch shut onto dry rock, the hoots and stoke of the early session forgotten. It ebbs and it flows.

« This is the magic of the coast; the tide brings it to life and then kills it. »

There's this other little place that barely exists. A remote cove, it only breaks a few times a year when the elements conspire. To even think about surfing it, you need a roaring westerly and a large long-period swell from a specific direction. Finally, and most importantly because without it the wave just thumps against a cliff, you need a huge spring low. The range between low and high tide changes with the lunar cycle. When the range is largest, the tides are called 'springs,' when it is smallest they are 'neaps.' Springs will usually occur two days following a full or new moon. This is the magic of the coast; the tide brings it to life and then kills it, and for all most people know, it was never even there at all.

The raging tides that flood Cornish beaches are very different to those in other areas of the world. For instance, the sometimes-lucky Mediterranean surfing community has one less element to worry about when the other elements conspire. Their tides are very low amplitude, and are a matter of centimetres rather than metres. This tidal discrepancy exists throughout the world, with each ocean having its own tidal system.

Once, a north coast retreat developed twin banks that became nicknamed 'the boobs.' Two conical humps of sand protruding, exposed by the low tide. As the water began to cover them, buoyed up by the force of the pushing tide, identical A-frames would form, spinning lefts and rights. They lasted a week, groomed by offshores and the tides,

and then a northwesterly destroyed them. You lose and gain.

Our tides are semi-diurnal, which means that we have two high and low waters over a 24-hour period. The largest tides of the year occur in line with the equinoxes. The 21 March is the Vernal Equinox, and the 23 September is the Autumnal Equinox. The semi-diurnal force of the tide is maximised, and extreme tides are more common. This occurs when the moon and sun are in line with the earth, and at their closest. Learning about the tides in your local area will develop an affinity with the place. As a surfer, you appreciate the beach, how the tide and wind affect the swell, what the rise and fall of the water does as it crosses each metre of sand. This anticipation is a privilege that comes about through feeling, seeing and doing.

« Compared to some parts of the world, Cornwall's tides seem small: the Bay of Fundy in New Brunswick, Canada, receives tides in excess of 15 metres. »

Those sessions when you meet someone else dripping wet with a mammoth grin as you dash to catch the tide, arriving to find the beach submerged and flat, begin to become less frequent. You start to put yourself in the right place at the right time. Being in the water as low tide turns and pushes the swell through the roof, when those rarely-covered reefs flicker alive for a few hours, or just as that fickle lefthander finally cranks. Knowing when and where to be to maximise the fun.

As surfers, we will become aware of rising sea levels sooner than most. The highest of the years' spring tides are already testing the resilience of sea defences, particularly when accompanied by storm surges. Who can say what rising sea levels will do to our beaches and reefs over time? The risks of coastal flooding are becoming higher. The environment is changing before our eyes. The rise and the fall of the tides, so integral to the Cornish surfing experience, covers the footprints that get thicker and heavier each year. +

cornish**oasis**.com

01. AGAPANTHUS   02. MAGNOLIA   03. FATSIA   04. PIERIS   05. CORNISH ROSE   06. BANANA PLANT   07. FAN PALM   illustration: jenny bowers

5

www.e-sidersurf.co.uk

LOOSE FIT

Loose-Fit T-shirts are made from 100% organic cotton - farmed, manufactured and printed under fair trade agreements. They are produced to the highest standard and printed using Soil Association accredited organic inks.

Conventional cotton farming is one of agriculture's most environmentally destructive activities. It takes an enormous toll on the earth's air, water, and soil, and significantly affects the health of people living in cotton growing areas.

A single typical conventional cotton t-shirt uses about 150 grams of acutely toxic pesticides and insecticides; that's the size of a cup of sugar (source: Soil Association). A Loose-Fit garment uses none.

Not only is organic cotton better for the environment but the end result is a really soft, comfortable and hard wearing garment. And, naturally, your skin can't absorb any toxic pesticides when you wear organic cotton clothing.

Loose-Fit is committed to helping our environment in every aspect of our business from using locally sourced recycled papers to planting trees in our own forest to offset the carbon footprint generated by our products and activities. We are a long standing member of the organisation 1% For The Planet as well as being the only carbon neutral surf enterprise in the world.

This catalogue has been printed on 100% post consumer recycled paper using non-GMO soy based inks. All designs are © Loose-Fit 2006.

Ordering info

Internet: **www.loose-fit.co.uk**

Phone: **01271 314549**
7 days a week - 10am to 6pm

Email: **info@loose-fit.co.uk**

Post: Send a cheque with your order & contact details to:

Loose-Fit,
Upcott Avenue,
Pottington Business Park,
Barnstaple,
EX31 1HN

please make your cheque out to Loose-Fit Ltd and write your cheque guarantee number on the back.

In Person:
We'd love to see you in the shop (address above). A cup of tea awaits.

If you are a shop and would like to stock Loose-Fit Organic clothing, please email **trade@loose-fit.co.uk**

LOOSE FIT

6

Organic Clothing 2006

THE DNA COMPETITION 06 HAS STARTED

DEADLINE: 15 TH JUNE 2006

DIESEL NEW ART SUPPORTS NEW TALENTS WITHIN ART, DESIGN, FILM AND PHOTOGRAPHY.

JUST GO TO WWW.DIESEL-NEW-ART.COM AND SUBMIT YOUR WORK.

More information:
contact@diesel-new-art.com
www.diesel-new-art.com

diesel new art

BLEED | OSLO, NORWAY
Bleed collective

Blurring the borders between graphic design, art and commercial brand identity, Bleed has made a visible place for itself in the world of design since 2000. The Oslo based outfit employs 14 people and its projects span from art exhibitions, identity design for major international brands and books to running their own concept store.

www.bleed.no

1 Diesel New Art competition poster | Diesel, 2006
2 Catalogue and logo | Alu Spa, 2007
3 Visual identity | Oslo Philarmonic Orchestra, 2007
4 Illustrated magazine spread | Bleed magazine, 2007
   Illustration by Kahori Maki
5 Campaign and identity | Arkaden Shopping Mall, 2006
6 Poster installation | Going Underground, 2007

NO
OT
WAY

LEAVE
YOUR
MARK

ALU

LEAVE
YOUR
MARK

2

KAHORI+BLEED

We are proud to be able to do a collaboration spread in our magazine with the works of Kahori Maki.
We met thru friends and now we are friends. Kahori showed us around Tokyo and we are forever grateful for a fantastic time.
Enjoy her marvelous illustrations and make sure to visit her web page at www.k-maki.com.

１９６８年生まれ。９２年日本大学芸術学部卒業後、渡米
Art Student League of NYにてファインアートを学ぶ。94年帰国後フリーランス
に。
一現在、イラストレーションを中心に、空間演出、絵画制作に力を入れている。

Born in Japan, 1968. Studied Fine Arts at the Art Student League of NY
(NYC, USA) following graduation from Nihon University's art department in
1996. As senior freelancer since her return to Japan in 1994, she has
produced a wide variety of illustration, installation and painting works.

EMIL KOZAK | BARCELONA, SPAIN
Emil Kozak

Emil Kozak began developing his design skills from an early age inspired by skateboard art and it shows in his work –the style is fresh and positive, yet there is always an unexpected obscure reference seething underneath. His work has been exhibited widely in Europe and the US and appeared in publications such as IDN and Victionary's Logology.

www.emilkozak.com

1 Self-promotional image | Self-initiated, 2006
2 CD artwork | Philip Braunstein, 2006
3 Posters | Sonja, 2007
4 Mag Awards prizes | Mags.dk, 2007

2

4

MAG AWARDS PRESENTED BY MAGS.DK

MagAwards 2006 Årets magasin

KBH

#01

4

EMILY FORGOT | LONDON, UK
Emily Alston

Emily Alston graduated from the Liverpool School of Art and Design and relocated to London where she works as a graphic designer and illustrator under the name Emily Forgot. She approaches her work with wit, originality and humour, and her many projects stretch across to printed textiles and ceramics as well as print.

www.emilyforgot.co.uk

1 Illustration for calendar | Self-initiated, 2005
2 Vinyl record sleeve design | Idle Lovers, 2006
3 Invite | Aboud Sodano for Paul Smith, 2004
4 Promotional posters | The Oxymorons, 2006
5 Illustration | If You Could publication, 2007
6 Plates and prints | 6 Exhibition, 2007
7 Illustration | Self-initiated, 2006

A.DECLARE YOUR INTEREST

AA.FOOTBALL SPECIAL

THE IDLE LOVERS

3

making things that don't go together go together

THE
OXYMORONS

LOCAT	
DATE	
TIME	

making things that don't go together go together

THE
OXYMORONS

LOCAT	
DATE	
TIME	

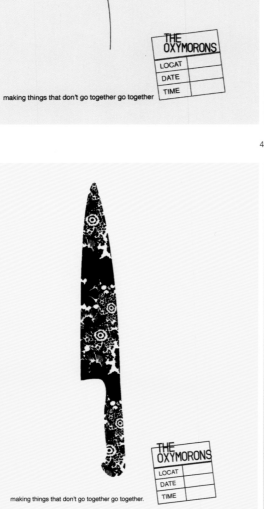

making things that don't go together go together.

THE
OXYMORONS

LOCAT	
DATE	
TIME	

making things that don't go together go together

THE
OXYMORONS

LOCAT	
DATE	
TIME	

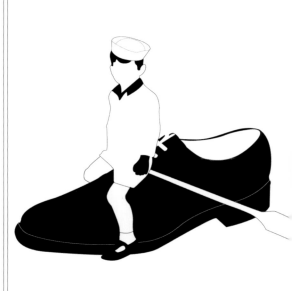

ditched

ISSUE 2
FREE

EMMABOSHI | BOLOGNA, ITALY
Emanuele Centola

After working with Pablo, a Bologna-based design studio where he was taught to swim between the muddy waters of the graphic design world, Emanuele Centola started his own freelance graphic design experience in 2004 under the name Emmaboshi, a portfolio for his solo projects while working between private clients and design studios.

www.emmaboshi.net

1 Magazine cover and poster | Ditched magazine, 2005
2 Illustration | Iceberg festival, 2005
3 Exhibition posters and flyers | Luciano Poli, 2007
4 Exhibition catalogue | Francesco Cocco, 2006
5 Illustration | Iceberg festival, 2005

LA BESCIAMELLA HA TANTE VARIANTI

FRA TUTTE LE SALSE TRADIZIONALI DELLA CUCINA, LA BESCIAMELLA È CERTAMENTE LA PIÙ IMPORTANTE E LA PIÙ DUTTILE. SI PRESTA INFATTI A MOLTI USI: POTETE UTILIZZARLA PER COMPLETARE LA COTTURA DI UN PIATTO O PER ACCOMPAGNARE MOLTI ALTRI, O PER DELIZIARE EMMABOSHI.

LUCIANO
POLI strati
24marzo2007orel8⁰⁰
imola | palazzo monsignani
via emilia 69

djset deepalso homework records
allestimento spada+ziveri, poli allestimenti
grafica emmaboshi www.emmaboshi.net

la mostra resterà aperta fino al 30 marzo
presso la libreria palazzo monsignani
lun-sab 9⁰⁰-12³⁰/15³⁰-19³⁰

PALAZZO MONSIGNANI
LIBRERIA

LUCIANO
POLI strati
{in bookshop}
19maggio2007orel7³⁰
lugo | librerie.coop
il globo centro commerciale
via foro boario 30

la mostra sarà aperta dal 15 al 26 maggio 2007
con i seguenti orari: lun 14⁰⁰-20⁰⁰/mar—sab 9⁰⁰-20⁰⁰

3

PRISONS FRANCESCO COCCO

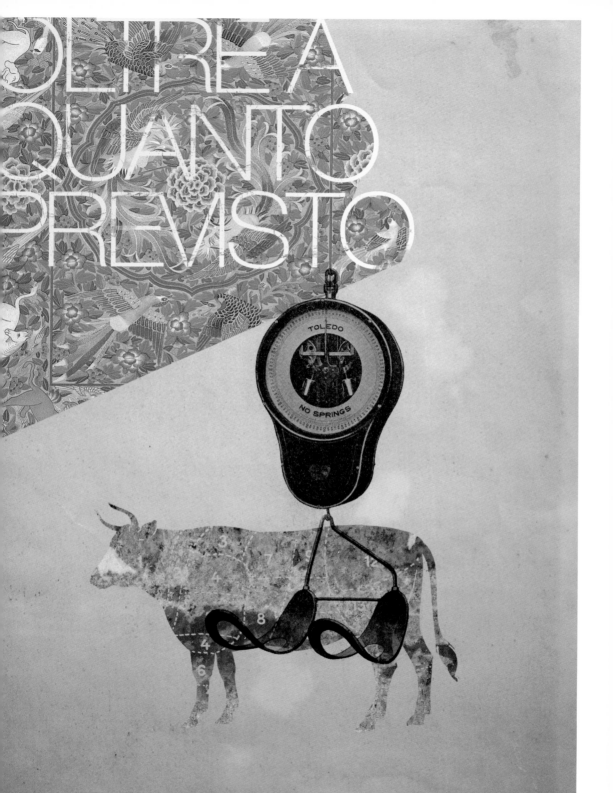

OLTRE A
QUANTO
PREVISTO

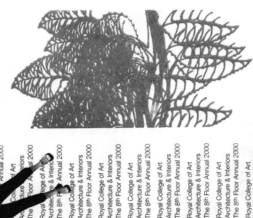

Royal College of Art
Architecture & Interiors
The 8th Floor Annual 2000
Royal College of Art
Architecture & Interiors
The 8th Floor Annual 2000
Royal College of Art
Architecture & Interiors
The 8th Floor Annual 2000
Royal College of Art
Architecture & Interiors
The 8th Floor Annual 2000
Royal College of Art
Architecture & Interiors
The 8th Floor Annual 2000
Royal College of Art
Architecture & Interiors
The 8th Floor Annual 2000
Royal College of Art
Architecture & Interiors
The 8th Floor Annual 2000
Royal College of Art
Architecture & Interiors
The 8th Floor Annual 2000
Royal College of Art
Architecture & Interiors
The 8th Floor Annual 2000

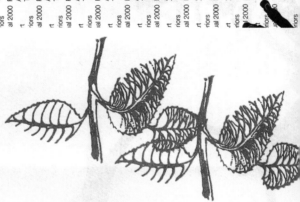

Royal College of Art
Postgraduate Art & Design

ERIC & MARIE | PARIS, FRANCE
Éric Gaspar, Marie Bertholle

Éric and Marie teamed up in 2002 but have worked together since the early days of graphic design school, having both studied at Central Saint Martins and the Royal College of Art in London. Each of their projects seeks to develop a different, singular approach to graphic design, experimenting in every stage from conception to production.

www.ericandmarie.com

1 RCA Architecture Catalogue | Royal College of Art, 2001
2 Book on George Sand | Culturesfrance, 2004
3 Letterpress prints | Self-initiated, 2000
4 Brochure | Sandra Musy, 2002
5 A Story of Graphic Design in France cover | Les Arts Décoratifs and Carré éditions, 2005
6 RCA architecture catalogue | Royal College of Art, 2001

BÉATRICE-DIDIER

George Sand

adpf ministère des affaires étrangères ●

« Comme créatrice de chefs-d'œuvre, vous êtes la première de toutes les femmes, vous avez ce rang unique, vous êtes la première femme, au point de vue de l'art, non seulement dans notre temps, mais dans tous les temps ; vous êtes le plus puissant esprit, et aussi le plus charmant, qui ait été donné à votre sexe. Vous honorez, Madame,

3

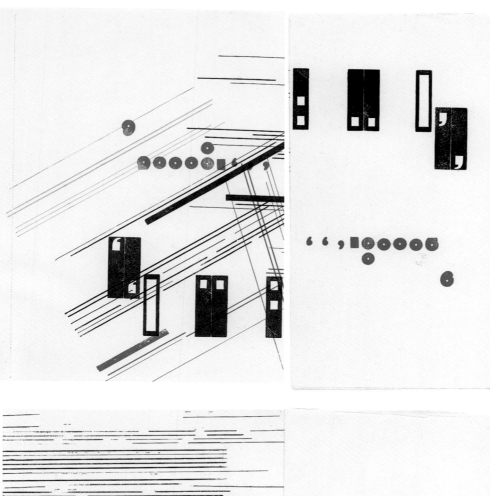
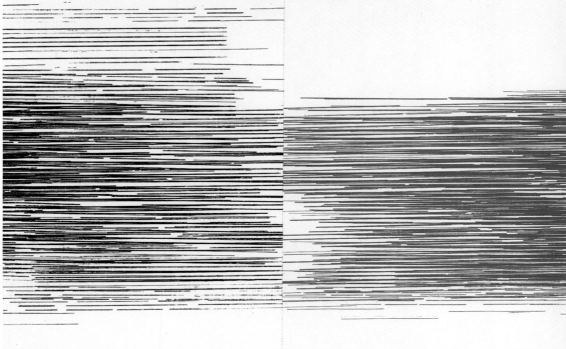

5

ERICA JACOBSON | STOCKHOLM, SWEDEN
Erica Jacobson

Ever since graduating from Konstfack University College of Arts, Craft and Design Erica Jacobson has been collecting awards and nominations on a yearly basis thanks to her fresh and colourful work in the fields of graphic design and illustration. Her work has been exhibited at the Liljevalchs Art Gallery in Stockholm and the Glaspavillon in Berlin.

www.ericajacobson.com

1 Promotional poster | The City Theatre of Stockholm, 2005
2 Book cover | Tiden, 2005
3 Promotional poster | The City Theatre of Stockholm, 2004
4 Identity and stationary | The Anna Lindh Memorial Fund, 2007
5 Promotional poster | The City Theatre of Stockholm, 2003
6 Promotional poster | Albert Bonnier, 2006

NICOLAS JACQUEMOT

PUSS!

Vad är egentligen kärlek?
Hur vet man om man är kär i någon?
Och hur vet man om den andra är kär tillbaka?
Hur frågar man chans? Kan man vara ihop
med flera samtidigt? Hur ska man göra slut?
Kärlek – så funkar det! ger dig svaren.

Är du kär?-test

Kysskola

Kärleksordlista

Flörtskola

Jag vill vara ihop
med dig!
//LINUS

TIDEN

KÄRLEK

SÅ FUNKAR DET!

ISBN 91-29-65442-9
9 789129 654429

NICOLAS JACQUEMOT

KÄRLEK SÅ FUNKAR DET!

anna lindhs minnes fond

anna lindhs minnes fond

anna lindhs minnes fond

anna lindhs minnes fond

Drottninggatan 83
S-111 60 Stockholm
Phone +46 8 411 90
Cell +46 706 10 90 91
Fax +46 8 411 92

info@annalindhsminnesfond.se
www.annalindhsminnesfond.se
PG 90 12 10-5
Org.nummer 90 12 10-5

anna lindhs minnes fond

Maria Enekvist
Organisationssekreterare

Drottninggatan 83
S-111 60 Stockholm
Phone +46 8 411 90
Cell +46 706 10 90 91
info@annalindhsminnesfond.se
www.annalindhsminnesfond.se

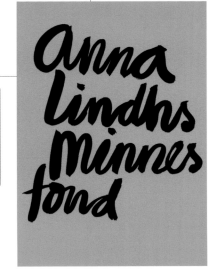

anna lindhs minnes fond

4

500 kcal

ALBERT BONNIERS FÖRLAG

LAPHROAIG SINGLE ISLAY MALT SCOTCH WHISKY

43%vol

Håkan Larsson
Om konsten att
äta och dricka

ANTOINE+MANUEL BY FL@33 2006

FL@33 | LONDON, UK

Agathe Jacquillat, Tomi Vollauschek

London based FL@33 was founded by Agathe Jacquillat and Tomi Vollauschek after they graduated from the Royal College of Art in 2001. Their work philosophy is based on the "Power of 3" theory that balances intellect, skill and emotion, and it shows in their vibrant and artistic projects whether they be commissioned or self-initiated.

www.flat33.com

1 FL@33 vs Antoine & Manuel poster | Two Faced project, 2006
   In collaboration with idN magazine,
2 Front cover design | Novum: World of Graphic Design magazine, 2004
3 Illustrations for Design & Designer 33: FL@33 monograph | Self-initiated, 2005
   Published by Pyramyd Editions
4 Visuals for Woyzeck print campaign | Young Vic theatre, 2005
5 Big Ask Live concert programmes and pledge cards | Friends of the Earth, 2006
6 Illustration for book and promotional postcards | Self-initiated, 2003 and 2006
7 Commissioned illustrations | Computer Arts magazine, 2006

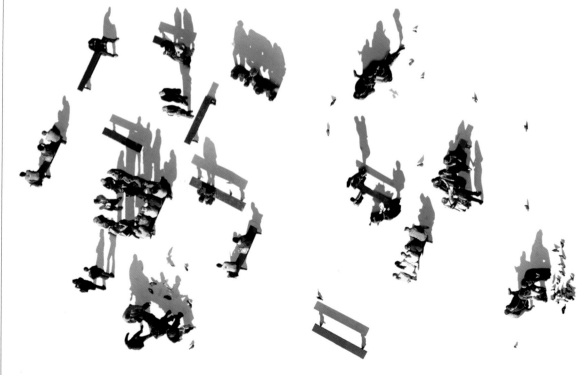

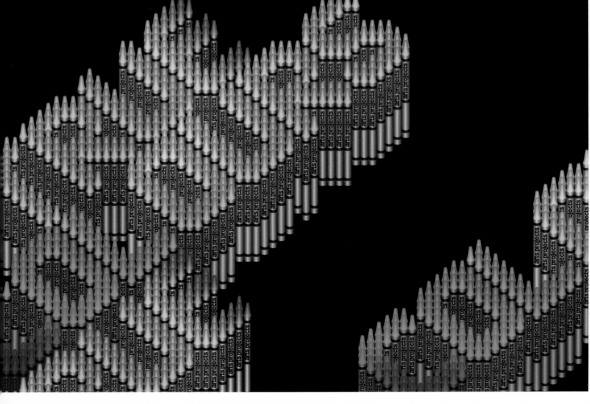

AIRS DE PARIS

FRÉDÉRIC TESCHNER | MONTREUIL, FRANCE
Frédéric Teschner

Frédéric Teschner graduated from the École Nationale Supérieure des Arts Décoratifs in Paris in 1997 and started working with Pierre Di Sciullo before joining the Atelier de Création Graphique in 1999. Since 2002 he has developed his work as an independent graphic designer, frequently collaborating with architects, designers and choreographers.

www.fredericteschner.com

1 Air de Paris invite | Pompidou Centre, 2007
2 Signage | Journées du Patrimoine la Valette-du-Var, 2006
3 Faits d'Hiver festival program | Faits d'Hiver festival, 2007
4 Promotional poster | Design-Métiers d'Arts, 2006
5 Invite | Villa Noailles Association, 2006
6 Promotional publication | Journèes du Patrimoine la Valette-du-Var, 2006
7 Hors Commerce box set and exhibition promotional publication | Editions Centre National des Arts Plastiques, 2007
8 Promotional poster | Pascal Montrouge Company, 2007
9 Airs de Paris exhibition catalogue and display tarpaulin | Pompidou Centre Editions, 2007

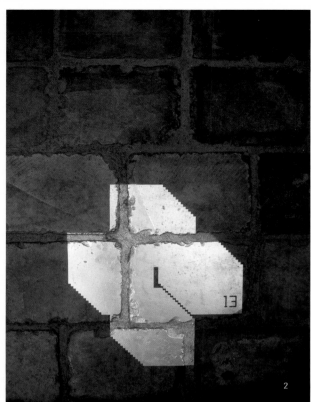

2

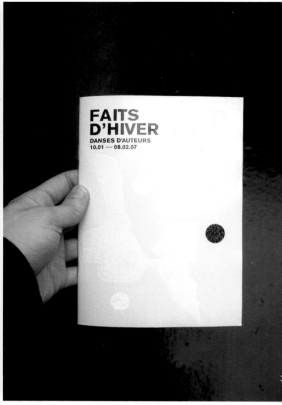

ÉRIC POITEVIN / MATHIEU LINDON

SARKIS / FRÉDÉRIC BOYER

ETTO / PATRICK GRAINVILLE

GILLES BARBIER / NATHALIE QUINTANE

PHILIPPE COGNÉE / PAUL FOURNEL

JACQUES MONORY / TANGUY VIEL

BERNARD DUFOUR / JACQUES HENRIC

ANNE FERRER / MARIE DARRIEUSSECQ

JEAN-LUC MOULÈNE / MANUEL JOSEPH

VALÉRIE FAVRE / MARYLINE DESBIOLLES

BRUNO SERRALONGUE / FRANÇOIS BON

FRANÇOIS CURLET / CHLOÉ DELAUME

HORS
COM —
MERCE

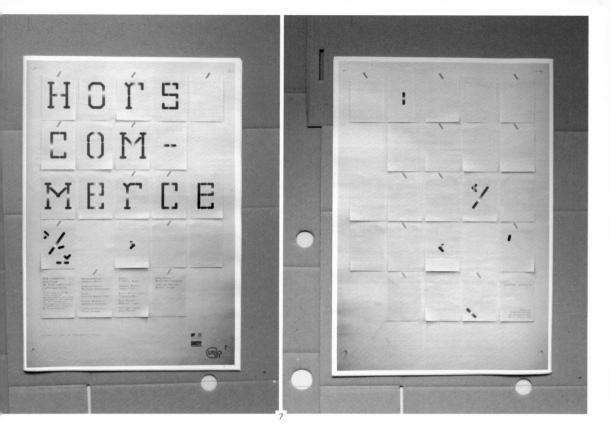

9

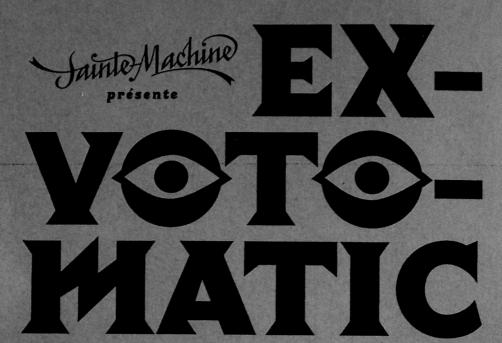

Sainte Machine présente

EX-VOTO-MATIC

— une exposition collective avec —

Kbanditta • Fanny Garcia • Jack Usine
John Bobaxx • Havec • Kolona • Pulko
Christophe Bouvet • Priscille Claude

30 juin → 15 juillet 2006
VERNISSAGE : VENDREDI 30 JUIN • 19H

GALERIE ARTEMIS

4, rue de l'engin, Eymet (près de Bergerac)

renseignements : 06.87.69.00.86 / benoit.lavaud@free.fr

www.sainte-machine.com

GARCIA USINE STUDIO | BORDEAUX, FRANCE
Fanny Garcia, Jack Usine

Fanny Garcia and Jack Usine founded Garcia Usine studio in Bordeaux after graduating from L'École des Beaux-Arts in 2005. It was conceived as a creative and experimental workspace, and alternates between work commissions, organising exhibitions and personally initiated projects such as Smeltery, the studio's own typographical division.

www.gusto.fr

1   Ex-voto-matic exhibition flyer | Sainte-Machine collective, 2006
2   Illustrated postcard | Arc en Rêve architecture centre, 2005
3   Soupirs à la Bordelaise project poster | Smeltery, 2005
4   Flyer, Le Vilain, 2006
    In collaboration with Kolona
5   Invite | Bordeaux School of Fine Art, 2007
6   Flyer | Sainte-Machine collective, 2006
7   Invite | Bordeaux School of Fine Art, 2007
8   Promotional poster | Artigues City Hall, 2007
9   Poster | Sainte-Machine collective, 2006
10 Poster | Marion Rebier, 2007

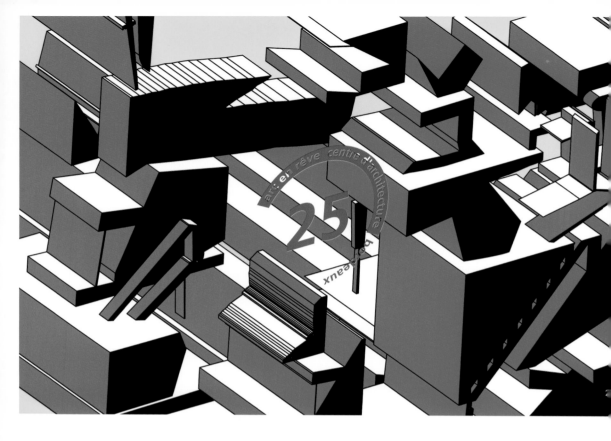

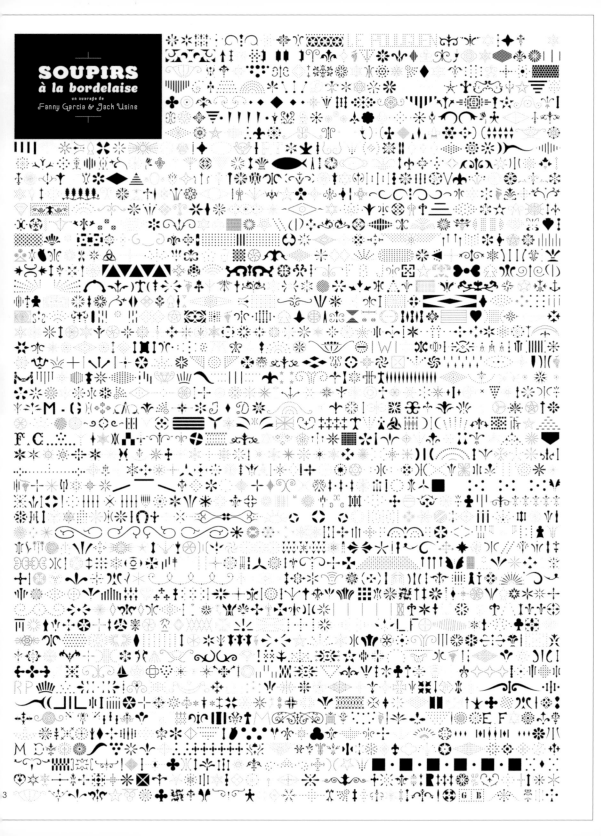

SOUPIRS
à la bordelaise

un ouvrage de
Fanny Garcia & Jack Usine

4

20 → 27 MAI 2006
SAINTE-FOY-LA-GRANDE
→ 17 rue Chanzy

VERNISSAGE
samedi 20 mai - 18ʰ

HORAIRES D'OUVERTURE
du 21 au 26 mai de 16h à 19h
samedi 27 mai de 10h à 19h

RENSEIGNEMENTS
06.73.77.97.93
www.levilain.org

4

5

Sainte Machine

présente

BUVONS
DU VIN !

une EXPOSITION COLLECTIVE
du 15 FÉVRIER au 5 MARS 2006

↳ merci Château Peneau !

avec

John Bobaxx
Christophe Bouvet
Fanny Garcia
Guillaumit
Havec
Kbanditta
Noam
Mr Kern
Jack Usine
..

VERNISSAGE
~pour la Saint-Valentin~
MARDI 14 FÉVRIER 19H

B.SHOP LA KOLONA

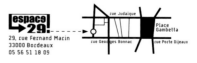

espace 29
29, rue Fernand Marin
33000 Bordeaux
05 56 51 18 09

imprim : les divines rotatives   –/–   ne pas jeter sur la voie publique

6

portes ou
vertes

MERCREDI 7 MARS 20

7 · 11H→18H **école de**

s Beaux-A

ts de Bord

eaux

ECOLE DES BEAUX-ARTS DE BORDEAUX

7, RUE DES BEAUX-ARTS
F — 33800 BORDEAUX
TEL +33 (0)5 56 33 49 10
bordeaux.fr

pot au CAFÉ POMPIER *à 18h*
7, place renaudel

journée

une expo photo de
Marion Rebier

////// 1e PARTIE //////

LA CENTRALE
15, rue Bouquière / Bordeaux

~~~~~~~~~

**DU 15 AVRIL
AU 15 MAI 2007**

~~~~~~~~~

vernissage

samedi **14 AVRIL**

→ à partir de **19H**

+ + + + + + + + + + +

+ **CONCERT**
de **Milla Rayen**

chansons d'Amérique Latine

+ + + + + + + + + + +

Contacts : lacentrale.bordeaux@free.fr / 05.56.51.79.16 & marionrebier@hotmail.com

graphisme → Garcia Usine studio • www.gusia.fr/// imprim Rodriguez

CIP
CENTRE INTERNATIONAL DE PERCUSSION
PRÉSENTE

SCULPTEURS DE SONS

CONCERT DE PERCUSSIONS ET MULTIMEDIA

DANSE

PIERRE JODLOWSKI
ET LES PERCUSSIONS DU CIP

SAMEDI 10 FEVRIER 2007 À 20H30
SALLE DU PALLADIUM, 3 BIS RUE DU STAND, GENÈVE

INFORMATIONS ET RESERVATIONS:
T: 022 329 85 55 // info@cipercussion.ch // www.cipercussion.ch

Avec le soutien du Département des Affaires culturelles de la Ville de Genève et le département des Affaires culturelles de l'Etat de Genève.

GVA STUDIO | GENEVA, SWITZERLAND
Alban Thomas, Gérald Moulière, Hervé Rigal

GVA Studio is a small company established in Geneva since 2004 who works for both private and institutional clients. Book and magazine design, art direction, packaging, web design and corporate identity as well as event and exhibition design are all accomplished in GVA's trademark style: bold and practical with a playful twist.

www.gvastudio.com

1 Promotional image | International Centre of Percussion, 2007
2 L'eau à la bouche exhibition catalogue and promotional material | Alimentarium museum, 2006
3 Buttercup Metal Polish CD packaging | Buttercup Metal Polish, 2006
4 Corporate identity | Group8 architects, 2006
5 CH Magazine issue 04 | Creatio Helvetica magazine, 2004

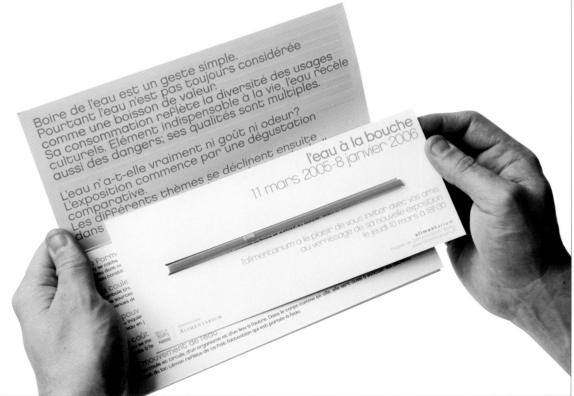

132

BUTTERCUP METAL POLISH
BUTTERCUP MP WORKS ON SEMI STRUCTURED AND
STRUCTURED IMPROVISATION WITHOUT CLEAR REFERENCES
TO ANY PARTICULAR GENRE IN A MAN/INSTRUMENT
CONTINUUM, IN WHICH SKIN AND METAL INSTRUMENTS
AS WELL AS OTHER TYPES OF MUSICALLY CONDUCIVE
MATERIALS ARE USED TO CREATE SOUND; BRINGING
TOGETHER ELEMENTS FROM DIFFERENT MUSICS IN A
DEFINED LIBERTY. THE DRUM KITS USED AS A STARTING
POINT ARE EXTENDED AND TRANSFORMED IN ALL KINDS OF
WAYS TO ENABLE THE POSSIBILITY OF THE DESIRED SOUND
AND IN THAT WAY ARE EVOLUTIVE, CONSTANTLY CHANGING
AND EVEN SELF MADE IN OCCASIONS.
USING TECHNIQUES LIKE FRICTION, RUBBING AND
SCRATCHING AS WELL AS THE USUAL "BANG THE DRUM"
THEY DEAL WITH THE ... NICE OR UGLY-
WITHOUT AEST... RESTRICTIONS
ONCE THEY ...
INTERAC... NDS.
PUTTIN... O ONE
DUO. ...
THE S... TO
RAN... W
ALL... LEVEL OF U...

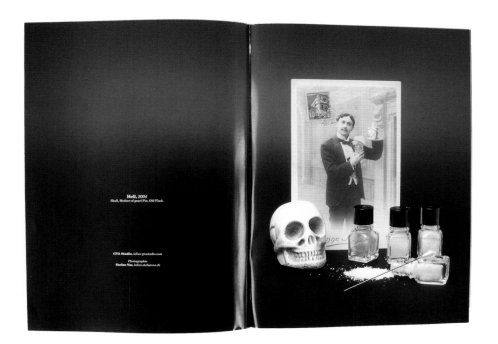

Hell, *2004*
Skull, Mother-of-pearl Pin, Old Flask.

GVA Studio, infos@gvastudio.com

Photographie
Stefan Vot, infos@stefanvot.ch

Paradise, *2004*
Keep Cool and be Gay Range, Gold and Mother-of-pearl Chest.
Silver Fish Stick.

HANS GREMMEN | AMSTERDAM, THE NETHERLANDS
Hans Gremmen

Hans Gremmen was born in 1976 in Langenboom and currently works as a freelance graphic designer based in Amsterdam. Despite his young age he has amassed an impressive and refined body of work, awards and exhibitions, and teaches in the graphic design and photography departments at St. Joost Academy of which he is also a former student.

www.hansgremmen.nl

1 Art Print | Iris Bouwmeester, 2007
2 Newsletters, Imago book and annual reports | Zeeuws Museum, 2003/07
3 Promotional posters | Muzieklab Brabant, 2004
4 Prints | Uitgeverij Lecturis, 2004
5 Invite | Hotel Mariakapel, 2007
6 Fw magazine | Photographers Platform, 2005/06
7 Black Hole book | Jaap Scheeren and Anouk Kruithof, 2006

'04

'04

JAAR-
VERSLAG
ZEEUWS
MUSEUM

05

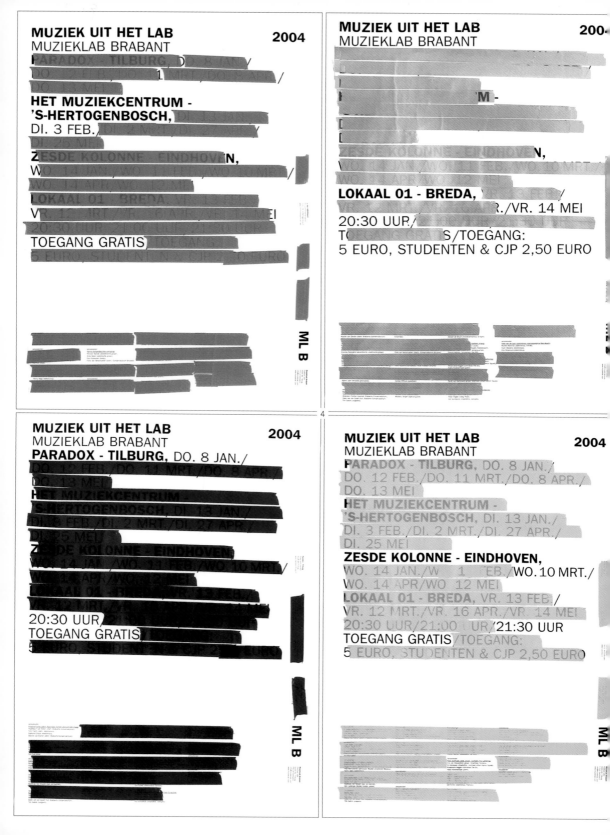

MUZIEK UIT HET LAB
MUZIEKLAB BRABANT

2004

PARADOX - TILBURG, DO. 8 JAN./
DO. 12 FEB./DO. 11 MRT./DO. 8 APR./
DO. 13 MEI

**HET MUZIEKCENTRUM -
'S-HERTOGENBOSCH,** DI. 13 JAN.
DI. 3 FEB./DI. 2 MRT./DI. 27 APR./
DI. 25 MEI

ZESDE KOLONNE - EINDHOVEN,
WO. 14 JAN./WO. 11 FEB./WO. 10 MRT./
WO. 14 APR./WO. 12 MEI
LOKAAL 01 - BREDA, VR. 13 FEB./
VR. 12 MRT./VR. 16 APR./VR. 14 MEI
20:30 UUR/21:00 UUR/21:30 UUR

TOEGANG GRATIS/TOEGANG:
5 EURO, STUDENTEN & CJP 2,50 EURO

ML B

MUZIEK UIT HET LAB
MUZIEKLAB BRABANT

200

LOKAAL 01 - BREDA,
/VR. 14 MEI
20:30 UUR/
TOEGANG GRATIS/TOEGANG:
5 EURO, STUDENTEN & CJP 2,50 EURO

MUZIEK UIT HET LAB
MUZIEKLAB BRABANT

2004

PARADOX - TILBURG, DO. 8 JAN./

20:30 UUR/
TOEGANG GRATIS

ML B

MUZIEK UIT HET LAB
MUZIEKLAB BRABANT

2004

PARADOX - TILBURG, DO. 8 JAN./
DO. 12 FEB./DO. 11 MRT./DO. 8 APR./
DO. 13 MEI
**HET MUZIEKCENTRUM -
'S-HERTOGENBOSCH,** DI. 13 JAN./
DI. 3 FEB./DI. 2 MRT./DI. 27 APR./
DI. 25 MEI
ZESDE KOLONNE - EINDHOVEN,
WO. 14 JAN./W 1 EB./WO. 10 MRT./
WO. 14 APR/WO 12 MEI
LOKAAL 01 - BREDA, VR. 13 FEB./
VR. 12 MRT./VR. 16 APR./VR. 14 MEI
20:30 UUR/21:00 UUR/21:30 UUR
TOEGANG GRATIS/TOEGANG:
5 EURO, STUDENTEN & CJP 2,50 EURO

ML B

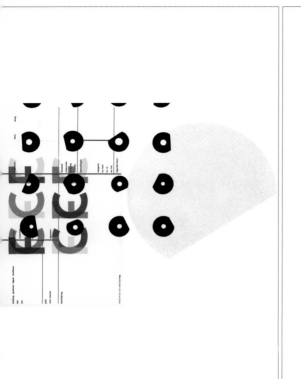

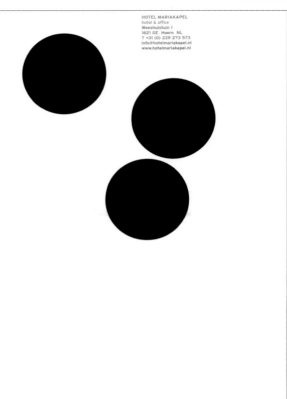

HOTEL MARIAKAPEL
hotel & office
Weeshuistuin 1
1621 GE Hoorn NL
T +31 (0) 229 273 573
info@hotelmariakapel.nl
www.hotelmariakapel.nl

5

Babette van Veen Kelder

Babette van Veen Grandioos

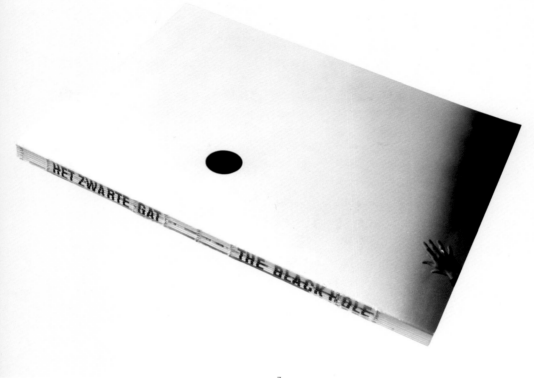

7

Nordic Music Days Iceland

**Festival of
contemporary music
October 5 – 14 2006**

**More info at
nordicmusicdays.is**

HÖRDUR LÁRUSSON | REYKJAVIK, ICELAND
Hördur Lárusson

Hördur Lárusson is a graphic designer from Iceland whose passion lies mostly in books and information design, although he has yet to combine the two. Since graduating from the Iceland Academy of the Arts in 2006 he has been awarded with a 2007 FIT design award and works at Atli Hilmarsson´s Atelier as well as on freelance projects.

www.larusson.com

1 Promotional poster, programme, postcards and buttons | Nordic Music Days Iceland music festival, 2006
In collaboration with Siggi Orri Þórhannesson and Sól Hrafnsdóttir
2 Propaganda poster | Self-initiated, 2005
3 Promotional poster | Ekka dance group, 2007
4 Promotional poster | Breakbeat.is, 2006
5 Vika book | School project, 2005
6 Bukk book | Self-initiated, 2005
7 Bullseye calendar | Self-initiated, 2007

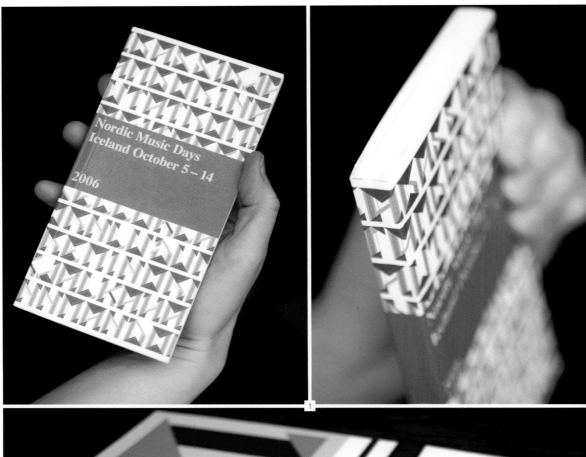

John B
[Beta Recordings, Metalhedz]

Breakbeat.is
Heineken
kynna:

NASA
föst. 29. sept
kl. 23.00

Kalli & Ewa
[Breakbeat.is]

Agzilla / Downtempo Special
[Metalheadz, Reinforced]

1000 kr. í forsölu
1500 kr. við hurð

Forsala í
12 Tónum
Skólavörðustíg &
Smekkleysubúðinni
Klapparstíg.

breakbeat.is   ★ Heineken

Hödelberg
Druckmaschinen
AG AD-30

Hödelberg
Druckmaschinen
AG AD-30

Gersemar
Kolaportsins

Kolaportið er frábær staður. Þessi illa lyktandi flóamarkaður, sem aðeins er opinn um helgar, er sennilega eitt af því skemmtilegra sem fyrirfinnst í Reykjavík. Að fara þarna er ævintýri í sjálfu sér. Manni líður sins og maður sé að róta í bílskúrnum hjá ömmu og afa í leit að einhverjum gömlum gullmolum. Þarna finnur maður meðal annars ballkjólana hennar ömmu, skipamódelin hans afa, 80's plöturnar hennar hábbu, Afríkustytturnar hennar mömmu, gamla He-man dótið sitt og allt þetta gagnslausa drasl sem maður man eftir úr æsku. Mitt í öllu draslinu rekst maður öðru hverju á gersemar. Eitthvað sem maður hélt að væri löngu týnt og tröllum gefið, eitthvað sem þig dreymdi um sem barn en fékkst aldrei, eða eitthvað sem þú vissir ekki einu sinni að þig vantaði fyrr en þú sást það. Á meðan maður gramsar er hægt að gæða sér á alls konar kræsingum. Kolaportið er jafnvel hörðum fiski, línum kókosbollum eða öðru undarlegu lostæti sem þarna fæst. Á sunnudögum er skemmtilegast er að skoða bókabásana. Pyfíkt magn af alíslkonar bókum veit það sem mér finnst boðið upp á mesau í kaffiterfunni. Myndi vilja sjá Kringluna keppa við það. Það sem mér finnst spottris! Naldi mér t.d. í þrjú sintbk af Birting frá 1963 sem Hörður Ágústsson hannaði og skrifaði í Þrjú stykki á 300 kall. Eftir þessi ánægjulegu ferð í Kolaportið fór ég og keypti mér loksins The Hitchhiker's Guide to the Galaxy eftir Douglas Adams. Löngu kominn tími á að lesa hana og það verður eiginlega að þrýst áður en myndin kemur.

THE
POEM
IS
THE
POEM

JEFF RAMSEY

ICE CREAM FOR FREE | BERLIN, GERMANY
Oliver Wiegner

ICE CREAM FOR FREE is a Berlin based design studio founded in 2005 by Oliver Wiegner. Having developed from a collective, the studio has access to a multidisciplinary team of designers, the main focus being on print and a special interest in illustration. Bubbling with ideas and an individual approach to design, ICE CREAM FOR FREE is ready to go.

www.icecreamforfree.com

1   Promotional poster | Self-initiated, 2006
2   Flyer | Hive Club, 2007
3   Flyer | Milch, 2007
4   Illustrations | Anda, 2007
5   Vynil record packaging | Flash, 2007
6   Poster | Licht magazine, 2007
7   Illustration | Self-initiated, 2006
8   Illustration | Latex for fun project, Max-o-matic, 2007
9   Flyer illustration | Milch, 2007
10   Poster | Coordination-Berlin, 2006

FLASH LABEL NACHT

SAMSTAG 24/03/07
AB 23 UHR
HIVE CLUB
GEROLDSTRASSE 5
8005 ZÜRICH

HIVECLUB.CH
MYSPACE.COM/FLASHREC

hive flash

DESIGN BY ICECREAMFORFREE.COM
FLIP FOR DJS

HIVE CLUB

OLIVER KOLETZKI
STIL VOR TALENT / FLASH / COCOON BERLIN

FLORIAN MEINDL
STIL VOR TALENT / FLASH / TRAPEZ LONDON

DON RAMON
SAN MARCO
MIKKY B
ELI VERVEINE
CHRISTO
TOBI DREIPOL

FLIP FOR INFO

2

BPITCH CONTROL CAMPING TOUR

DISCO
KIKI
BPITCH CONTROL/BERLIN

TOMAS ANDERSSON
BPITCH CONTROL/STOCKHOLM LIVE!

SMASH TV
BPITCH CONTROL/BERLIN

ANIMAL TRAINER
AKA ADRIAN FLAVOR & RX

TANZSTUBE / cheeknchong / AFTERHOUR AB 7 UHR
DON RAMON / SAN MARCO
RINO / PASCI / BANG GOES
JAUSS

SAMSTAG   **HIVE CLUB**
08/04/07   **GEROLDSTRASSE 5**
AB 23 UHR   **8005 ZÜRICH**
                            HIVECLUB.CH

hive bpc
cheeknchong

DESIGN BY
ICECREAMFORFREE.COM

WAS TRINKT DIE KUH?
AM MITTWOCH 16/05/2007
AB 22 UHR
ROSI'S/REVALER 29/FHAIN

DJ FLASH DANCE A.K.A.
JAN DELAY

MONTOUA
LIVEDEMO

VELTENMEUER
MILCH

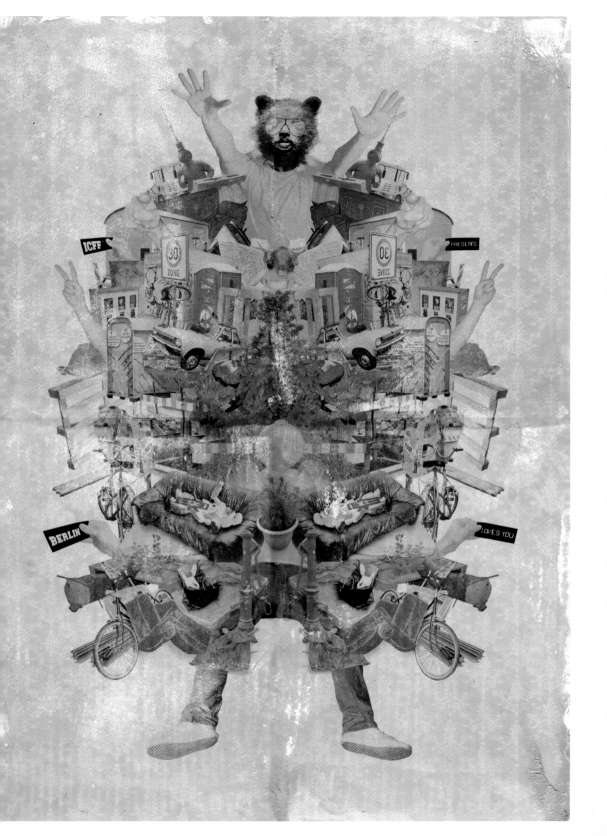

JAN KALLWEJT | WARSAW, POLAND
Jan Kallwejt

Jan Kallwejt was born in 1981 in Warsaw. His studies in advertising led to jobs as designer and art director at various internet companies as well as interactive and design agencies, and after being kept busy for two years at Fork Unstable Media in Hamburg he has decided to start working freelance with a special focus on illustration.

www.kallwejt.com

1 Illustration | PolenPlus magazine, 2007
2 Logos | MaMa foundation, Bolzplatz and OSTA organization, 2005/06
3 Illustration | Beautiful/Decay magazine, 2005
4 Promotional illustration | 2nd records, 2006
5 Badge designs | Self-initiated, 2005
6 Tee shirt design | Beautiful/Decay magazine, 2007
7 Illustrations | Hiro magazine, 2006

MaMa

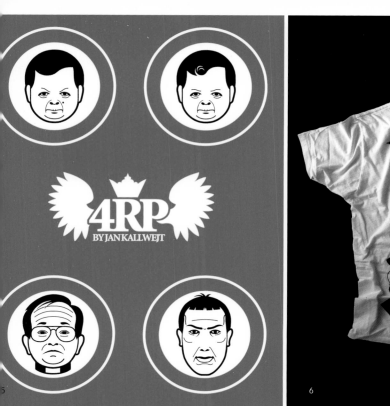

5

6

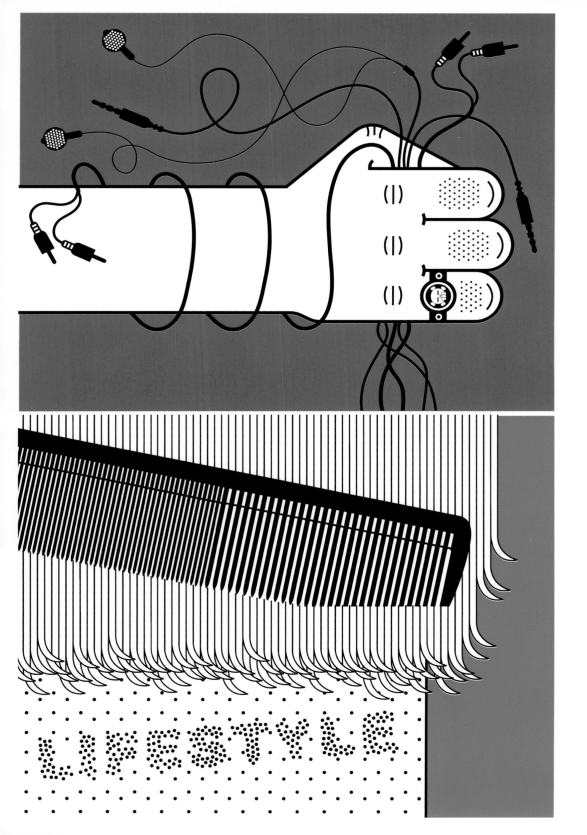

KATRIN KAUFMANN | BERN, SWITZERLAND
Katrin Kaufmann

Katrin Kaufmann was born in Basel, Switzerland in 1982. After studying graphic design and illustration at the Schule für Gestaltung in Biel she moved to Berlin and worked at Hendrik Schwantes's studio for 8 months. She currently attends the University of Bern and works as a freelance graphic designer between Bern and Berlin.

www.katrinkaufmann.ch

1 Digital and hand-drawn collage | Self-initiated, 2005
2 Postcards and folder | Perspektiven und Praxis, 2005
  In collaboration with Lea Willimann
3 Illustration | Self-initiated, 2005
4 Typeface and booklet | Self-initiated, 2006
5 Annual report | Schule für Gestaltung Bern, 2003
  In collaboration with Violaine Walther, Sonja Hugi, Rachel Bloch
6 Masculinites catalogue | Neuer Berliner Kunstverein, 2005
  In collaboration with Hendrik Schwantes

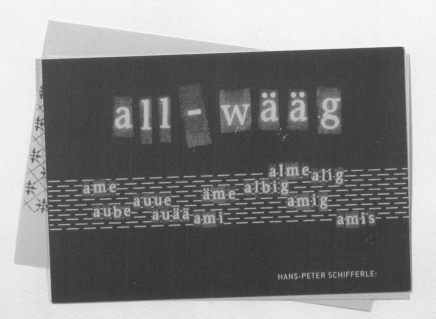

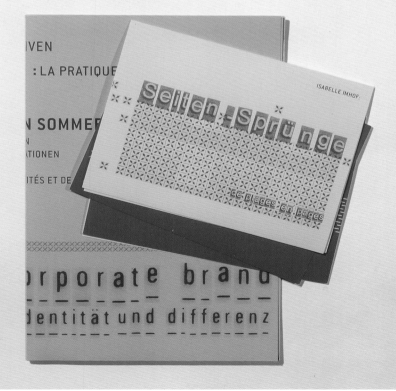

NICHT VERGESSEN!

SILEX FOR EVER

P SOIRÉE PRIMEUR   FREITAG, DEN 26. NOVEMBER 2004 À 17 HEURES 30

JCKBLICKE - FUNDSTÜCKE - UND EIN PODIUMSGESPRÄCH -

LE 20ÈME NUMÉRO DE SILEX - ET UNE PUBLICATION SPÉCIALE

DAMALS WAREN WIR IN BERLIN

DER PAKT
10 13 179 19 74 14 11

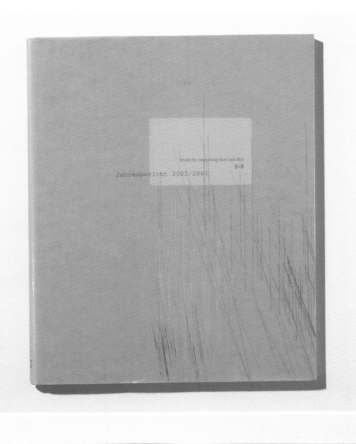

Schule für Gestaltung Bern und Biel
B:B
Jahresbericht 2002/2003

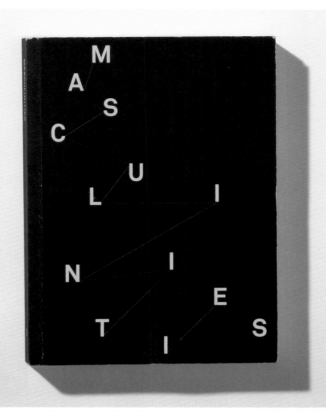

DOGTROEP

Poster

Poster for a performance held at a new ho
development that was still under constru

Client: **Dogtroep**
Year:

LAVA | AMSTERDAM, THE NETHERLANDS
Lava collective

Lava is a creative environment that has, as the name suggests, a burning passion at its core. Founded in 1990 in Amsterdam, Lava possesses a surprising and diverse design portfolio with recurring work in the area of editorial design and identity development, and their widespread client base ranges from the cultural to the corporate.

www.lava.nl

1 Promotional poster | Dogtroep, 2003
2 This Cover: 126 Magazine Covers self-published book | Self-initiated, 2006
3 Ode to the New Professional book | Vitae, 2006
4 Greeting cards | Vitae, 2007
5 Corporate identity | Impact festival, 2007
6 Corporate identity | The Roman Catholic Church of Holland, 2007

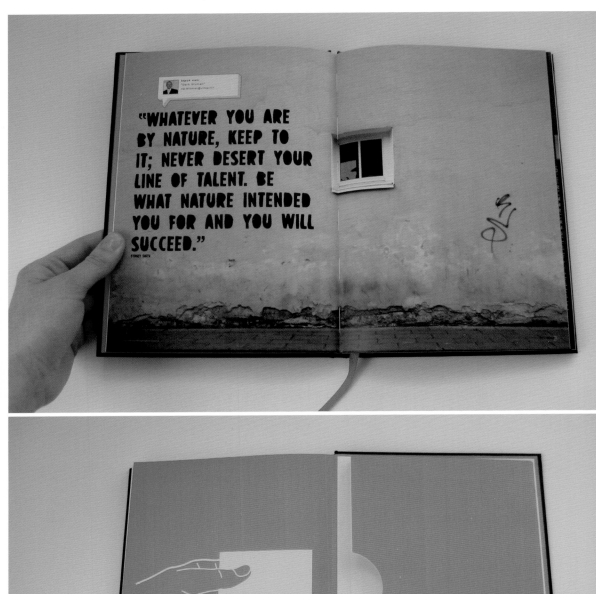

"WHATEVER YOU ARE BY NATURE, KEEP TO IT; NEVER DESERT YOUR LINE OF TALENT. BE WHAT NATURE INTENDED YOU FOR AND YOU WILL SUCCEED."

SYDNEY SMITH

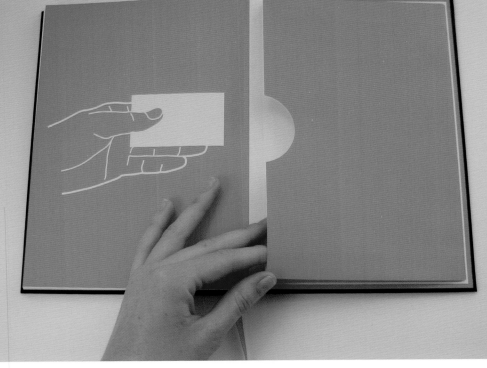

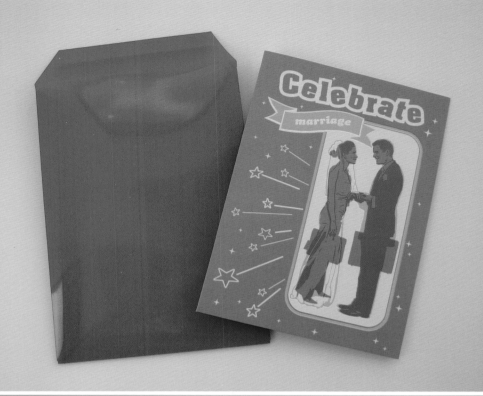

Streative
Fortunes For You

2007

LIKE | AMSTERDAM, THE NETHERLANDS

Edwin van den Dungen, Joey Kops

Like is an Amsterdam based graphic design duo working in the field of graphics, type and fashion. Their skill to provide clients with smart and exclusive look books, visual identity or brochures has won them clients like Nike and MTV, as well as giving workshops at the University of Applied Sciences and Arts in Lugano, Switzerland.

www.like.nl

1 Calendar booklet | Streative Branding, 2006
2 Calendar booklet spreads | Streative Branding, 2006
3 Booklet, Museum De Paviljoens | Yeb Wiersma and Vanessa Hudig, 2004
4 I Love exhibition poster | Koninklijke Academie van Beeldende Kunsten, 2007
5 We Make Art exhibition publication | Arti et Amicitiae, 2007
6 Promotional notebook | Streative Branding, 2006

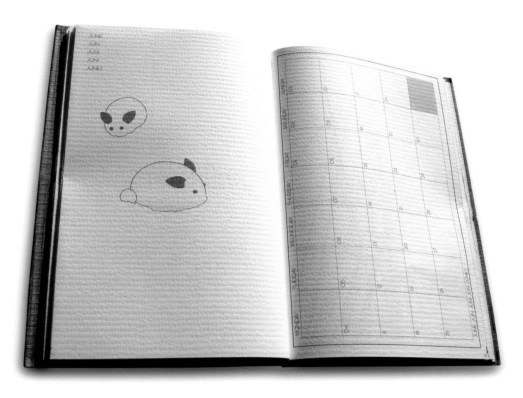

FORTUNE FAVORS THE BRAVE.

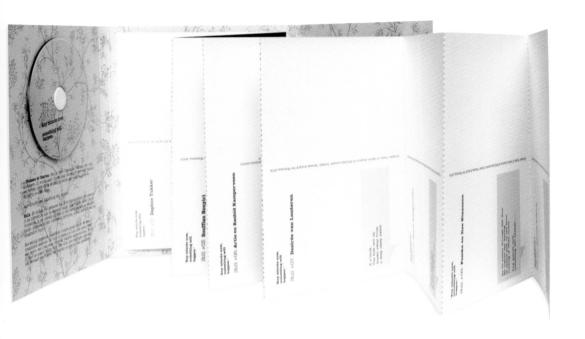

Een tentoonstelling van nieuw
werk gemaakt aan de Koninklijke
Kunstacademie door studenten en
oud-studenten van de School voor
Jong Talent

Opening en performance donderdag 11 jan 2007
om 16.30 uur (Toegang is gratis)

Tentoonstelling: 11 jan t/m 26 jan
Openingstijden: ma t/m vr van 10 tot 17 uur

Cultuurfonds

Kc   Kabk

PROJECT

Koninklijke Academie voor
Beeldende Kunsten in Den Haag
Prinsessegracht 4
2514 AN Den Haag

Design by Lille, /R

We Make
Art

Annemarie Bleeker   Theo Tomson

Ine Boermans   Casper Verborg

Marieke Coppens   Yilan Yuen

Klaartje Esch

Jachya Freeth

Petra Groen

Stephanie Jamet

Joost Nieuwenburg

Guido Nieuwendijk

Deborah Roffel

Eva Roovers

Anje Souid Roosjen

"Quotes are nothing but
an inspiration for the uninspired"
— Richard Kemp —

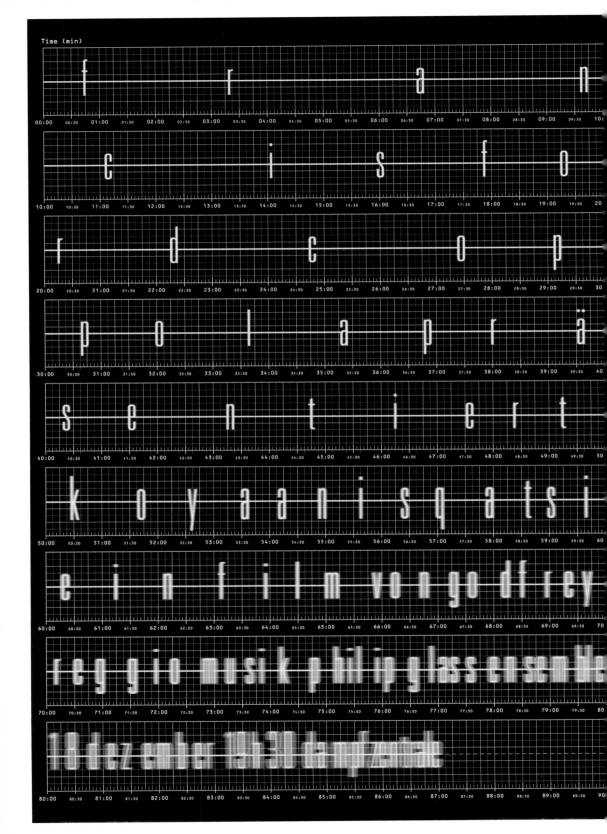

LORENZO GEIGER | BERN, SWITZERLAND
Lorenzo Geiger

Freelance Graphic and typeface designer Lorenzo Geiger lives and works in Bern, Switzerland, and specializes in web design, creating typefaces and producing printed matter, from logotypes to posters. After having worked for Philippe Apeloig in Paris and Fons Hickmann in Berlin, he graduated from the University of the Arts in Bern in early 2007.

www.lorenzogeiger.ch

1   Poster proposal | Koyaanisqatsi, 2004
2   Poster series proposal | Kunstvermittlung Kunsthalle Bern, 2006
3   Mapping:CH collection of maps | Graduation work, 2007
4   Promotional posters | Reitschule Bern, 2006

2

SAMSTAG, 7. JANUAR 2006 13H30
TREFFPUNKT BEI DER KUNSTHALLE. DAUER DES RUNDGANGS: 2H

LEITUNG: INES SCHWEINLIN, KUNSTVERMITTLUNG KUNSTHALLE BERN
ANMELDUNG: KUNSTHALLE BERN: 031 350 00 40 KUNSTHALLEBERN.CH

AUSSTELLUNG: 29. JANUAR BIS 26. MÄRZ 2006
ÖFFNUNGSZEITEN: MI - SO 10H - 17H, DI 10H - 19H

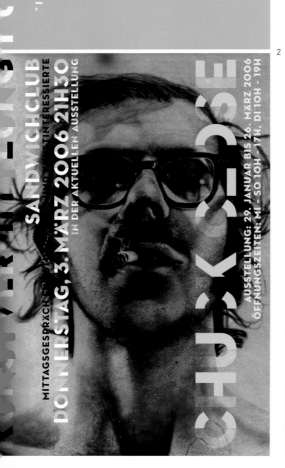

SANDWICHCLUB
MITTAGSGESPRÄCH FÜR ALLE INTERESSIERTE
DONNERSTAG, 3. MÄRZ 2006 21H30
IN DER AKTUELLEN AUSSTELLUNG

AUSSTELLUNG: 29. JANUAR BIS 26. MÄRZ 2006
ÖFFNUNGSZEITEN: MI - SO 10H - 17H, DI 10H - 19H

SANDWICHCLUB
MITTAGSGESPRÄCH FÜR ALLE INTERESSIERTE
DONNERSTAG, 3. MÄRZ 2006 21H30
IN DER AKTUELLEN AUSSTELLUNG

AUSSTELLUNG: 29. JANUAR BIS 26. MÄRZ 2006
ÖFFNUNGSZEITEN: MI - SO 10H - 17H, DI 10H - 19H

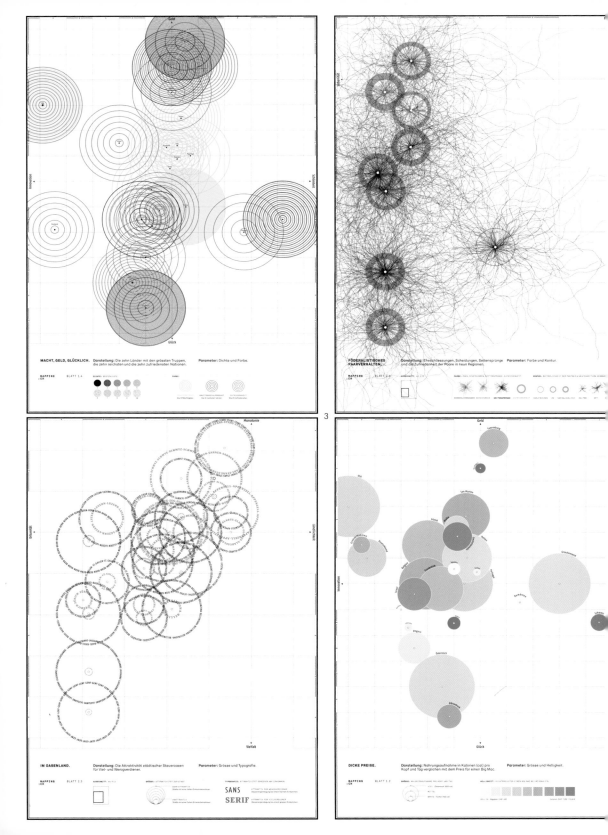

3

FROM PULVER RECORDS / BUDAPEST, HUNGARY

ERIK SUMO AND BAND

R REALISTIC WORLD MUSIC DANCEFLOOR SOUNDTRACKS   SUPPORTED BY DJ RINGMASTER

FRIDAY SEPTEMBER 29 TH **2006 DOORS 22H**
PRESALE AT ROCKAWAY BEACH, SPEICHERGASSE 35, BERN

ACHSTOCK REITSCHULE BERN

FROM NEW YORK CITY / USA

ROY NATHANSON'S SOTTO VOCE

AUM FIDELITY / N.Y.C.

ROY NATHANSON: AS, SS, VOC. (JAZZ PASSENGERS)
CURTIS FOWLKES: TB, VOC. (JAZZ PASSENGERS)
SAM BARDFELD: VIOLIN, VOC. (JAZZ PASSENGERS)
TIM KIAH: ACC. BASS, VOC. (ASTROGRASS)
NAPOLEON MADDOX: BEATBOXING, VOC. (ISWHAT?!)

JAZZ + POETRY = HIPHOP AND SWING

SUNDAY OCTOBER 29 TH **2006**
21H DACHSTOCK REITSCHULE BERN

4

LUKE BEST | LONDON, UK
Luke Best

Designer and illustrator Luke Best has managed to apply his way of image making to both commercial and personal projects. His diverse output, both as a solo artist and collaborative member of the Peepshow collective, includes video and animation, self published books, window displays, art direction and designing homemade spacesuits.

www.lukebest.com

1 Illustration | Self-initiated, 2007
2 Interactive children's book | Victoria and Albert Museum, 2006
3 Tee-shirt designs and visual identity | Brikabrak Records, 2006 / 07
4 Book project | Self-initiated, 2002
5 Illustrations for promotional book | Heart illustration agency, 2006
6 Self-promotion badges | Self-initiated, 2007

Islamic Middle East

You are now going to the Middle East, find the archway that leads into this gallery, Room 42

Are you getting thirsty? Turn left and find this picture made of tiles from Iran.

Can you see some bottles? Count how many different kinds there are in the picture

– – –

Pomegranate juice was a traditional drink in Iran. Talk about what kind of drinks you would like at your picnic.

Use this space to draw a ewer and write a recipe for a tasty drink inside it.

Your guests are getting hungry! Now goto the other side of the gallery and look for this Egyptian 'Mamluk' tray made of bronze, gold and silver.

Talk about what type of snacks will you carry on your tray. Use the word-search to help you decide.

dates	mint	cheese
nuts	hummus	biscuits
sultanas	cucumber	sandwiches
yoghurt	crisps	falafels
pitta	cake	samosas

O	H	U	M	M	U	S	B	S	S
N	R	B	L	P	Y	A	S	C	L
S	U	E	I	L	O	N	A	A	E
E	T	T	B	U	G	D	N	K	F
T	T	A	S	M	H	W	A	E	A
A	B	I	S	C	U	I	T	S	L
D	S	P	S	I	R	C	L	R	A
M	P	M	I	N	T	H	U	T	F
D	C	H	E	E	S	E	S	C	I
S	A	M	O	S	A	S	P	M	D

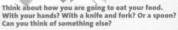

Think about how you are going to eat your food. With your hands? With a knife and fork? Or a spoon? Can you think of something else?

Next stop China, look out for some chopsticks.

Picnic Party

Family Trail

Japan

Go through the archway into Japan, Room 45. Turn right and look at the dishes in the cases.

Can you spot these dishes?, they show perfect picnic spots. A picture on a dish may help you decide where to have your picnic (in a garden, in a forest, under a waterfall?).

In the centre of this dish, draw the place where you would like to have your picnic and create a decorative Japanese pattern around the edge.

South Asia

Follow your map to find South Asia, Room 41

Look at the floor-cloths the people are sitting on in this painting and the one next to it, Draw a design for your own picnic rug inspired by the textiles found all over this room. Look around for plants, flowers, animals and birds to draw.

Look for this painting showing some Indian women enjoying a musical evening outdoors. It is next to the case of Mughal costume. They have a tray of snacks and drinks to enjoy as they play their instruments. Imagine the type of music or instruments you and your guests would like to listen to.

Talk about what you will eat at your picnic. Imagine that you are picking up your rug and moving into the Middle East gallery.

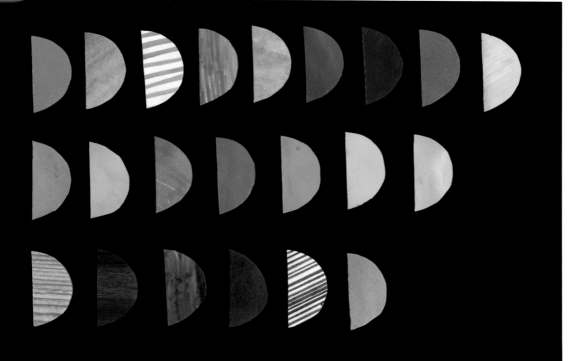

Death stands there in the background, but don't be afraid

NAROSKA DESIGN | BERLIN, GERMANY
Marc Naroska

Marc Naroska founded his Berlin based design studio in 2000. Naroska Design believes in the power of creative collaboration and combines analytical thinking with a passion for craft, having a strong national and international client base that includes the M100 Sansoucci Colloqium and the Federal Foreign Office in Norway and Germany.

www.naroska.de

1 Promotional posters | CO Berlin, 2006/07
2 Award, certificate and documentation brochure | M100 Sanssouci Colloquium, 2006
3 Magnum exhibition poster | CO Berlin, 2007
4 Brochures | CO Berlin, 2006/07
5 Cosmetics packaging | Michalsky, 2007
6 Packaging, shopping bag and product catalogue | Santaverde, 2006

Certificate

The M100 Sanssouci Award is hereby presented to

Bernard Kouchner

in recognition of his own personal services
to the cause of freedom and humanity
and as the directing spirit of "Medecins Sans Frontières"
by the board of the M100 Sanssouci Colloquium at Schloss Sanssouci.

Schloss Sanssouci, Potsdam, 8th September 2006

The Lord Weidenfeld of Chelsea

M100 SANSSOUCI COLLOQUIUM 2006

M00 SANSSOUCI
COLLOQUIUM

Mioo-Board

Jann Jakobs
chairman
Lord Weidenfeld
co-chairman

Stefan Aust
Boris Biancheri
Dr. Hugo Bütler
Kai Diekmann
Dr. Mathias Döpfner
Dr. Peter Frey
Dr. Alexander Gauland
Bodo Hombach
Hans-Ulrich Jörges
Dr. Josef Joffe
Baroness Kennedy QC
Hans Werner Kilz
Roger Köppel
Giovanni di Lorenzo
Alain Minc
Dr. Klaus Reinl
Thomas Roth
Dr. Rachel Salamander
Stephan Sattler
Dr. Frank Schirrmacher
Senator Karl Schwarzenberg
Dr. Wolfram Weimer

Moritz van Dülmen
executive director

Mioo-Office

Am Alten Markt 9
D-14467 Potsdam
Tel +49 331 2010-100
Fax +49 331 2010-111
contact@m100potsdam.org
www.m100potsdam.org

M00 SANSSOUCI
COLLOQUIUM

Miriam Weber

Am Alten Markt 9
D-14467 Potsdam
Tel +49 331 2010-100
Fax +49 331 2010-111
Mobile +49 179 23 63 108
m.weber@m100potsdam.org
www.m100potsdam.org

215

Hard labour shapes the work throughout the year and in particular the work of our labourers Pedro and Claudio. The soil is worked in accordance with regulations on controlled organic cultivation, and the plants are tended year round, exclusively by hand.

Harvest time commences following the sunniest month of the year: July. Pedro and Claudio select the ripe Aloe Vera leaves in the fields, and remove them by hand from the parent plant. To do this, each individual leaf is carefully scored and removed using physical strength, without damaging the parent plant.

Laid on top of one another in open boxes, the fresh leaves are sent straight on to be further processed.

Organic cultivation means taking one's time. Time, during which the plants can absorb vitality from the sun and soil. We aid natural soil regeneration by using exclusively vegetable preparations.

7.**TEATAR**FEST

Sarajevo, 22. - 26. 09. 2004.

NINA DESIGN | SARAJEVO, BOSNIA
Aleksandra Nina Knezevic

Aleksandra Nina Knezevic was born in Sarajevo and graduated from the Academy of Art in Cetinje, Montenegro. Her
work is fresh and contemporary, and easily communicates
an international visual language through playful typography
and graphics. Her projects have been awarded in design
festivals in Bosnia, Italy and Japan.

www.ninadesign.co.ba

1 Promotional poster | Sarajevo Theatre Fest, 2004
2 Postcards | Revival festival, 2006
3 Promotional poster | Sa Club, 2006
4 Missing book | Andrej Djerkovic, 2005
5 Sarajevo font | Self-initiated, 2007
6 Catalogue and promotional poster | Sarajevo Theatre
Fest, 2006/07

DARKWOOD
DUB

PETAK
24.mart

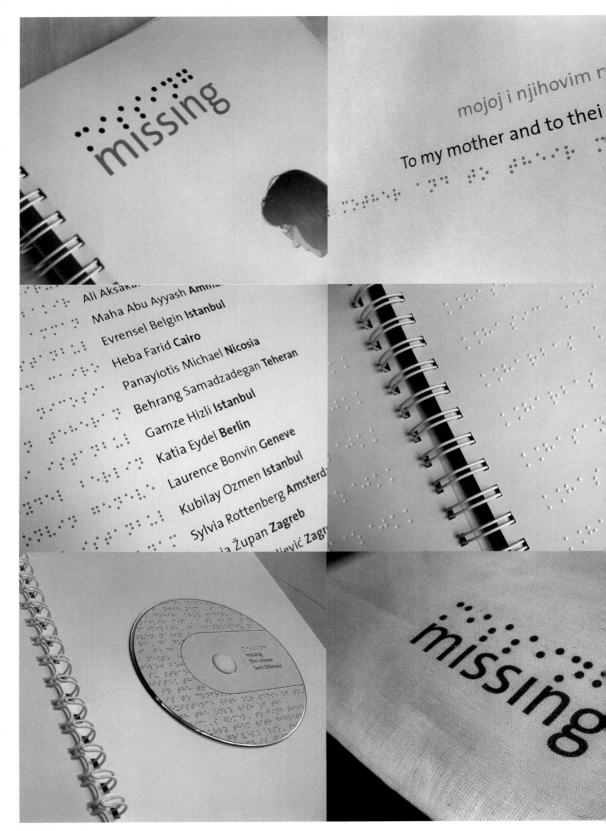

Sarajevo

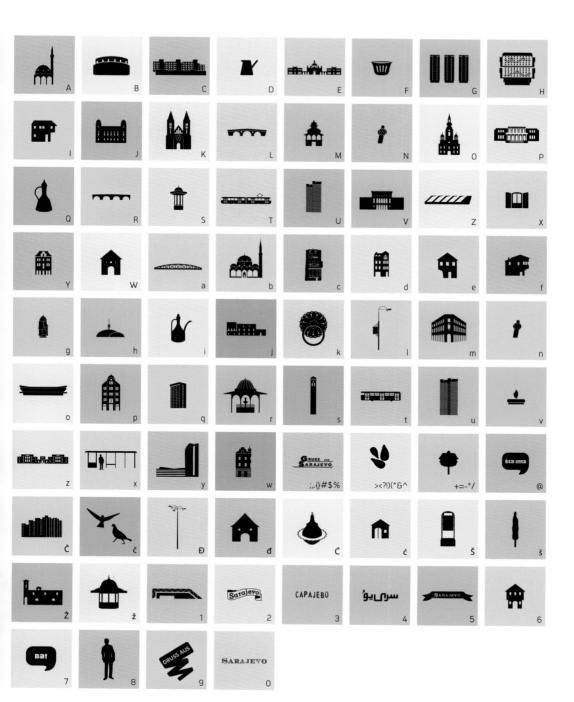

10.
teatar
FEST

www.tf.com.ba, info telefon: 033 442 958

Happy Days Sound Festival 2006
Oslo 5. – 8. april

Tema: Periferi

Georg Nussbaumer (AT):
Installasjon, video og performance

Operaen «Hvalen, eller Moby Dick»
av Bendik og Simen Hagerup

"Hjemme hos"
Eksklusive bussturer hjem til komponister

Serialisme på kjøpesentre

Egen Off-Happy Days Festival
med bla Oslo Filharmoniske Orkester

HAPPY DAYS SOUND FESTIVAL
Happy Days er en liten, grenseoverskridende
festival for lydbasert kunst.

Støttet av;
Norsk kulturråd
Fond for utøvende kunstnere
Operatoriet
Norsk Komponistforening

Happy Days arrangeres av
Ny Musikk
www.nymusikk.no

NODE | BERLIN, GERMANY/OSLO, NORWAY

Anders Hofgaarf, Serge Rompza,
Vladimir Llovet Casademont

Node is a graphic design studio based between Berlin and Oslo, which was founded in 2003 by Anders Hofgaard and Serge Rompza, Vladimir Llovet Casademont later joining the collaboration in 2006. All three studied at Gerrit Rietveld Academy in Amsterdam, and their prolific output includes books, typefaces, identities, signage and websites.

www.nodeberlin.com

1 Happy Days Sound festival posters | Ny Musikk, 2005/07
2 Stamm books | Götz Offergeld and Girault Totem, 2002/04
   In collaboration with André Wyst
3 Artist monograph | Antoni Tàpies Gallery, 2005
4 Artist's catalogue | Martina Schumacher and Kunstverein Arnsberg, 2007
5 Audio Alphabet typeface project | Ny Musikk, 2006
   In collaboration with Felix Weigand
6 Poster | Berlin China Cultural Bridge, 2006
7 Brochures | Bentvelsen Fleer Architectuur Stedenbouw, 2004
   In collaboration with Felix Weigand
8 Neighbours book | Loyens & Loeff, 2002
   In collaboration with Daphne Corell
9 Fort Island Ijmuiden book | Self-initiated, 2002
10 Magazine design | Mono Kultur, 2006
11 Magazine design | Juno Kunstverlag, 2004/07
12 Magazine design | Mono Kultur, 2006

1

Ny Musikk
www.nymusikk.no

NO-DO | NEUCHÂTEL, SWITZERLAND
Noémie Gygax, Yann Do

no-do is a Swiss graphic design studio founded by Écal University of Art and Design graduates Noémie Gygax and Yann Do. After respective internships at Baldinger in Paris and Practise in London, the design duo set up their studio in Neuchâtel, producing high quality print and illustration as well as typography and photography.

www.no-do.ch

1 Faits Divers bookcover | Self-initiated, 2005
2 Graphic design system developed for low-tech flyers | Self-initiated, 2006
3 Accélération exhibition poster and book | Kunstart, 2007
4 Illustration for vinyl record | DJ Maël C., 2006
5 Iasi Contemporary Art Biennale exhibition catalogue | Florence Derieux, 2006

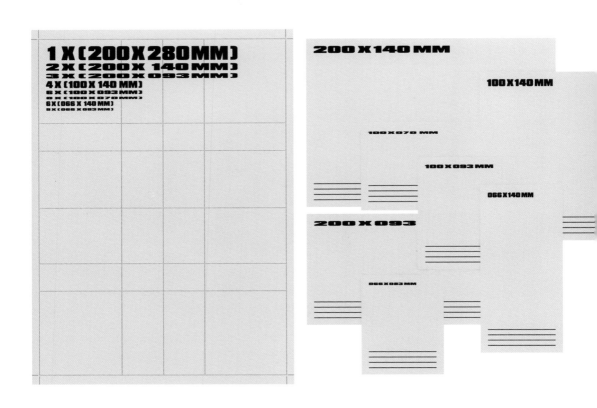

1 X (200 X 280 MM)
2 X (200 X 140 MM)
3 X (200 X 093 MM)
4 X (100 X 140 MM)
5 X (100 X 093 MM)
8 X (100 X 070 MM)
6 X (066 X 140 MM)
9 X (066 X 093 MM)

200 X 140 MM

100 X 140 MM

100 X 070 MM

100 X 093 MM

066 X 140 MM

200 X 093

066 X 093 MM

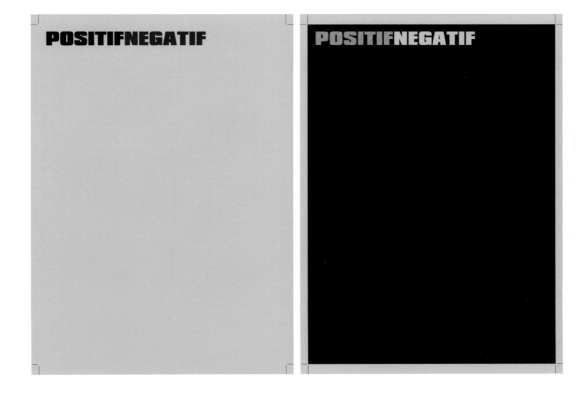

POSITIFNEGATIF

POSITIFNEGATIF

JEUDI 16 MARS 06 / [...]
ISH FOLKABILLY ROCK[...]
PERFECT'S JAMIE CL[...]
RK (IRL) EX-POGUES

ST-PATRICK DAY! IRISH FOLKABILLY ROCK!
JEU 16 MARS / CAVEAU DU KING / 21H00 / 12.–

WE LOVE JAZZ / JEUDI 06 AVRIL 06 / LEMI'S DIXIEL AND BAND

LA[...]
RO[...]
: C[...]
IN[...]
FE[...]
TR[...]
S)[...]
IR[...]
M[...]
RO[...]
CO[...]
VA[...]
EF[...]
RE[...] & PEDROLI (DRUMS)

**MARDI JAZZ[...]
DE MARS / M[...]
ARS: SAM B[...]
OMBONE) &[...]
BI (PIANO) / MARDI 21
MARS: INDIAN SUMM
ER: DANIEL SCHLAPPI
(CONTREBASSE) & THO
MAS SAUTER (GUITA
RE) / MARDI 28 MARS
ELINA DUNI (CHANT) &
COLIN VALLON (PIANO)**

JEUDI 16 FEVRIER 06
/ LECTURE MUSICALE
/ "FAUT-IL SAUVER P
EGGY SNEED?" & LES
REVES DES AUTRES"
JOHN IRVING (USA)

RECITANTE: SEVERINE FAVRE
INSTRUMENTISTE: NICOLAS HOINIGER

[...]R
[...]CK /
[...]CLA

JEUDI 06 AVRIL / BARKING / LEMI'S DIXIELAND BAND
REPAS DES 19H00 / LES CURRY DU KING / RESERVATION RECOMMANDÉE
CONCERT DES 20H00 / ENTREE LIBRE

BAR KING / DÈS 20H30 / ENTRÉE LIBRE (COLLECTE)

IRISH FOLKABILLY ROCK!
JEU 16 MARS / CAVEAU DU KING / 21H00 / 12.–

LES MARDIS JAZZ / BAR KING / DÈS 20H30 / ENTRÉE LIBRE (COLLECTE)

ARTISTES: DARREN ALMOND, KADER ATTIA,
MASSIMILIANO BALDASSARRI, FRANCIS
BAUDEVIN, DONATELLA BERNARDI, TOBIAS
BERNSTRUP, LILIAN BOURGEAT, DANIELE
BUETTI, COLLECTIF FACT, CHRIS CUNNINGHAM,
PHILIPPE DE CRAUZAT, WIM DELVOYE, LIONEL
FERCHAUD, FRED FISCHER, MASSIMO FURLAN,
PIERRE GATTONI, FABRIZIO GIANNINI, FABIEN
GIRAUD, LORI HERSBERGER, FRANÇOIS JAQUES,
VINCENT LAMOUROUX, ANNIKA LARSSON,
MATHIEU MERCIER, GEROLD MILLER, ELENA
MONTESINOS, SEBASTIAN MUNIZ, KARIM
NOURELDIN, XAVIER PERRENOUD, MATTHIEU
PILLOUD, HENRIK PLENGE JAKOBSEN, TILL
RABUS, JOËL VACHERON, PATRICK WEIDMANN,
MARTIN WIDMER, FRANCISCO DE MATA

13 MAI 07 –
30 JUIN 07

**CAN (CENTRE D'ART
DE NEUCHATEL)**
RUE DES MOULINS 3
2001 NEUCHATEL
+
**HALLE DE L'ANCIEN
KARTING (SUCHARD**
RUE DE TIVOLI 11
2003 NEUCHATEL-
SERRIERES

HORAIRES: MER=14H00–18H30 /
JEU=14H00–20H00 / VEN=14H00–18H30
SAM+DIM=12H00–17H00

APRES
L'ACCELERATION

Lorsque l'on parle d'accélération, on pense souvent au pilote de Formule 1 : il appuie sur le champignon et la force prodigieuse de son moteur le plaque contre son siège-baquet. Quiconque est déjà monté dans une Ferrari ou autre monstre propulsé par moteur à explosion a déjà expérimenté cette sensation étourdissante : le corps semble écrasé par son propre poids. Lorsque le skieur franchit le portillon de départ de la célèbre Streif de Kitzbühel, la descente la plus rapide et éprouvante du monde, il parcourt les premiers 100 mètres en moins de quatre secondes, une accélération comparable à celle d'une Porsche, modèle sport. Mais dans le cas du descendeur, l'accélération est produite non par des forces extérieures (un véhicule), mais par le propre corps du skieur, qui, s'il éprouve des forces pouvant aller jusqu'à 3G, ne ressent pas les pressions d'une accélération « subie ». « Tu ne la ressens pas parce c'est ta propre masse qui produit l'accélération et qui se déplace » précise un ancien coureur. Si sur la majeure partie de la course, le descendeur glisse sur la neige (ou le plus souvent sur la glace) en tentant d'opposer la moindre résistance au vent, il « tombe » véritablement sur le premier tronçon et joue avec les forces gravitationnelles (tout corps qui tombe est en état d'apesanteur). J'aime à imaginer que les spectateurs confrontés pour la première fois dans leur existence à un *ready-made* de Marcel Duchamp ont

on entend la foule, on sent sa présence 0 h 24' 45''

le son du bruit 0 h 24' 57''

on a l'impression que tout a été décidé 0 h 30' 47''

le scénario a déjà été écrit 0 h 30' 51''

quand les choses tournent mal 0 h 29' 19''

parfois on veut oublier 0 h 29' 56''

comme d'une expérience « en temps réel » 0 h 30' 14''

où quelque chose d'extraordinaire 0 h 16' 56''

est arrivé 0 h 16' 59''

je savais exactement ce qui allait se passer 0 h 57' 12''

1 h 01' 55''

1 h 01' 47''

1 h 01' 49''

1 h 01' 00''

1 h 02' 01''

1 h 02' 03''

1 h 02' 04''

1 h 02' 05''

1 h 02' 07''

1 h 02' 09''

parfois la magie ne tient pas à grand chose 1 h 25' 18''

1 h 25' 24''
en fait...

1 h 25' 30''
presque à rien

1 h 25' 31''

SIMON STARLING

Home made three-legged stool, 2001–2004.
These three hand-made platinum/palladium
prints depict a simple but lovingly crafted
three-legged stool found in Cluj, Romania.
This improvised, mobile support for the
body was made using a broom handle and
an old pair of jeans – all held together
with screws secured in home made washers
fashioned from 3 devalued Romanian coins.

Tabouret artisanal à trois pieds, 2001–2004.
Ces trois reproductions sur platine/palla-
dium, faites manuellement, montrent un
tabouret à trois pieds, simple, mais ravissant,
trouvé à Cluj, en Roumanie. Ce support
mobile improvisé a été réalisé à partir d'un
manche de balai et une paire de jeans usés
qui ont été assemblés à l'aide de vis fixées
dans des rondelles confectionnées de ma-
nière artisanale à partir de trois monnaies
roumaines hors d'usage.

Taburetul artizanal cu trei picioare, 2001–2004.
Aceste trei reproduceri pe platină/paladiu,
confecționate manual, înfățișează un taburet
cu trei picioare, simplu, însă încântător,
găsit la Cluj, România. Acest suport mobil
improvizat a fost realizat dintr-o coadă de
mătură și o pereche uzată de blugi, care au
fost asamblate cu ajutorul unor șuruburi
fixate în gaibe confecționate artizanal din trei
monede românești ieșite din circulație.

69–73

PETPUNK | VILNIUS, LITHUANIA

Andrius Kirvela, Gediminas Siaulys

PetPunk is the result of the collaborative efforts between Andrius Kirvela and Gediminas Siaulys. Respectively
brought up as an artist and as a programmer, both turned
to graphic design and creative advertising, joining forces to
form PetPunk in 2005 and specializing in graphic design,
illustration and video animation.

www.petpunk.com

1 Layout and illustration | Effigy, 2007
2 Logos, Accept & Proceed | Bang! magazine and
  Lithuanian Hip Hop Music Awards, 2007, 2006, 2007
3 Officer font | Self-initiated, 2007
4 Illustration and postcard | Next festival, 2006
5 Illustration on two-pillow set | PetPunk, 2005
6 Shopping bag | PetPunk, 2006

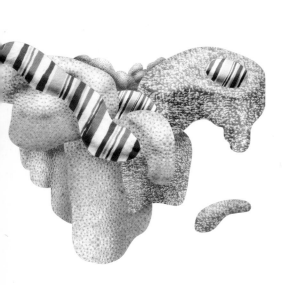

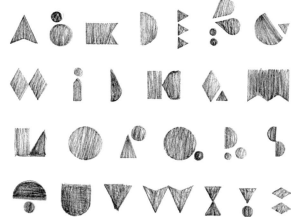

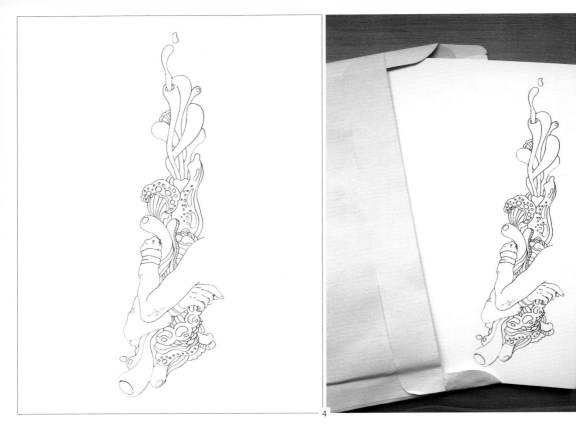

4

PLEASELETMEDESIGN | BRUSSELS, BELGIUM

Damien Aresta, Pierre Smeets

Pleaseletmedesign is composed of young graphic designers Pierre Smeets and Damien Aresta. Set up in 2004 after the duo graduated from Saint-Luc Higher School of Arts in Liège and spent time at Graphic Research School in Brussels, their inventive design projects cater to cultural sectors as diverse as music, architecture and advertising.

www.pleaseletmedesign.com

1　Programme | Court Circuit Association, 2006
2　Invite | ERG Graphic Research School, 2005
3　Catalogue | Label Architecture, 2006
4　CD package design | Funk Sinatra, 2007
5　Promotional buttons | Self-initiated, 2007
6　Identity | Playout records, 2007

SÉMIOLOGIE
ACTUALITÉ CULTURELLE
ANTHROPOLOGIE
PSYCHANALYSE
ESTHÉTIQUE
THÉORIE DES MÉDIAS & DE LA COMMUNICATION
SCIENCES ÉCONOMIQUES, POLITIQUES & SOCIALES
DROIT

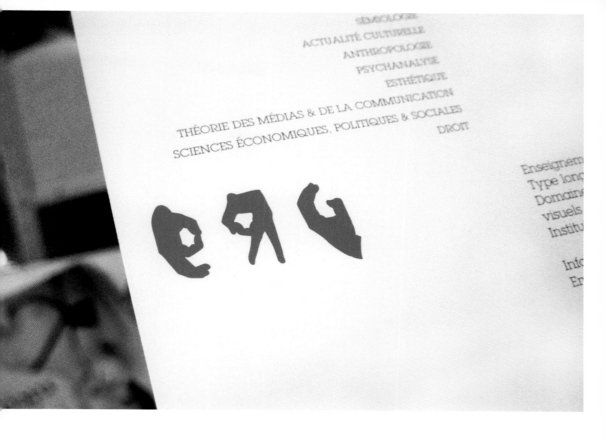

Enseignem
Type long
Domaine
visuels
Institu

Info
En

La
beauté
de
l'ordi-
naire

De comment je me suis disputé avec mon voisin

A16 & Label Architecture

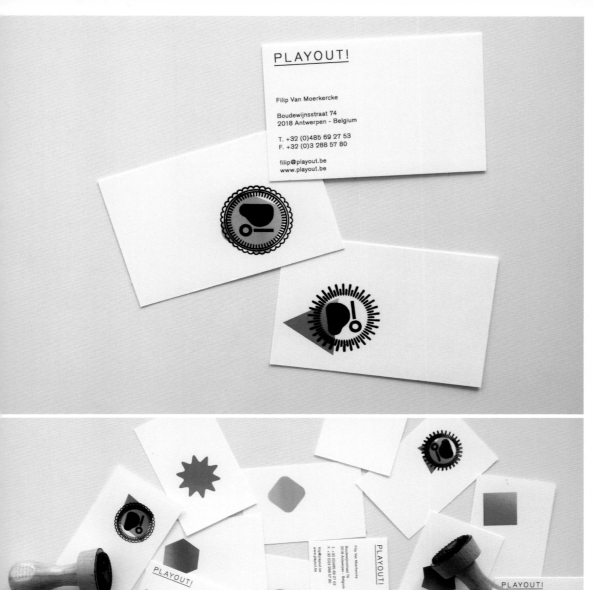

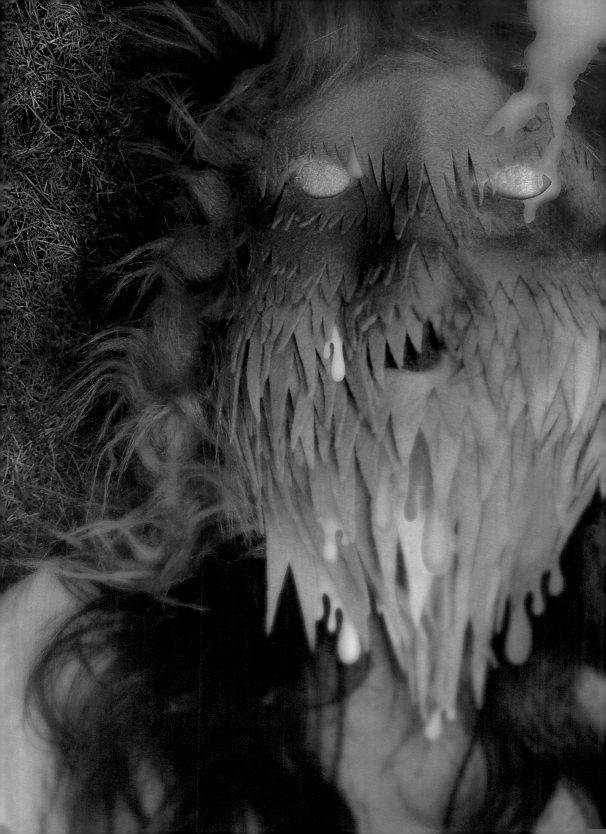

PMKFA | BORLÄNGE, SWEDEN
Micke Thorsby

Born in Sweden in 1979, designer Micke Thorsby, a.k.a. PMKFA, now resides in Tokyo after spending the first half of this decade in Copenhagen and London. Once heavily focused on music graphics, PMKFA is now also an art-director for the Swedish furniture brand Vujj as well as co-founder/designer of the clothing label It's Our Thing.

www.pmkfa.com

1 Illustration | Arkitip, 2005
2 Kocky CD packaging | La Vida Locash records, 2007
3 Product catalogue | Vujj, 2006
4 Illustration | Arkitip, 2005
5 Illustration | Hit n'Run magazine, 2004
6 Product catalogue | Vujj, 2006
7 Logos | Rickard Javerling, Wood Wood, Hairy Situation records, Yes King records, 2005/06

MOLLIS. PRODUCT FAMILY #1.

EASY CHAIR /COFFEE TABLE.

Mollis.
Easy chair.

(Design: Artur Moustafa & Jonas Nordgren.)

A visually lightweight and pleasingly proportioned piece, Mollis is a low-slung easy chair that revels in simplicity of form. The slender wooden seat is made from moulded veneer that curves around the body and is available with a stained or transparent lacquer finish. The seat pad is made from foam and is upholstered in either fabric or leather. The chair sits upon a double cross steel leg frame, available in either powder coated or satin chromed finish. The Mollis is an easy chair that delivers comfort and elegance in equal measure, suitably resolved to sit well at home or in contract environments.

Dimensions: 700 x 900 x 850h mm, seat height 370 mm.

Mollis.
Coffee table.

(Design: Artur Moustafa & Jonas Nordgren.)

The Mollis coffee table has a wooden tabletop a double cross steel leg frame, available in either powder coated or satin chromed finish. Designed as a companion piece to the easy chair, the table shares the inherent simplicity and lightness of form. It is also characterised by the large dimensions of the tabletop, making it ideal for larger reception areas and open plan domestic living.

Dimensions: 1250 x 700 x 450h mm.

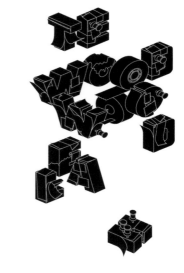

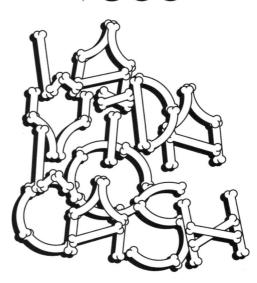

PROJECT GRAPHICS | PRISHTINA, KOSOVO
Agon Çeta

Agon Çeta was born in Kosovo in 1983 and graduated in architecture from the university of Prishtina in 2007. Project Graphics has been his creative portfolio since he first started working on design projects in early 1999, inspired by the emerging electronic music scene. Today Project Graphics also covers interior design and photography.

www.projectgraphics.net

1 Flyer | Multisound Connection, 2005
2 Digital art | Self-initiated, 2006
3 Flyer | Marco Lenzi, 2005
4 CD sleeve design | Fatos Äeta, 2005
5 Book cover | Skender Berani, 2007
6 Book cover | Doruntina Basha, Shkelzen Tuzi and
   Jeton Neziraj, 2006

contrast
fatos
çeta

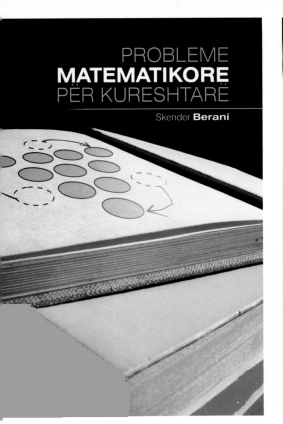

PROBLEME
MATEMATIKORE
PËR KURESHTARË

Skender **Berani**

Doruntina Basha
Shkelzen Tuzi
Jeton Neziraj

THE
FORBIDDEN
LESSON
a play for young people aged 12+

6

BREAKBEAT.IS

OG ★ Heineken® KYNNA:

ENDURKOMA BREAKBEAT.IS KVÖLDANNA

B

Á SKEMMTISTAÐNUM PRAVDA
FIMMTUDAGINN 10. FEBRÚAR
KL. 21:00 – 01:00

DJ KALLI
DJ LELLI
DJ GUNNI EWOK

18 ÁRA ALDURSTAKMARK
SKILRÍKI SKILYRÐI

FRÍTT INNI

RAGNAR FREYR | REYKJAVIK, ICELAND
Ragnar Freyr

Ragnar Freyr is a freelance designer from Reykjavik, Iceland, and operates a one-man graphic design and typography studio currently located in Michigan, USA. Initially a graduate in Sociology and Philosophy, he later attended the Icelandic Academy of the Arts from where he graduated in 2005 with a BA diploma in Graphic Design.

www.ragnarfreyr.com

1 Promotional poster | Breakbeat.is, 2006
2 Promotional poster | Breakbeat.is, 2005
3 Logos | NA, FRONT design studio and LED pencils, 2005/06
4 CD cover | Iceland-Palestine Association, 2005

Breakbeat.is & Heineken kynna: OLD SKOOL Laugardaginn 11. júní frá kl. 24:00
á Gauknum, Tryggvagötu. Maggi Lego, Frímann Psycho, Bjössi Brunahani.
500 krónur til kl. 02:00. 1000 krónur eftir kl. 02:00. 20 ára aldurstakmark.

★ **Heineken**

CHAPLIN

FR
ONT

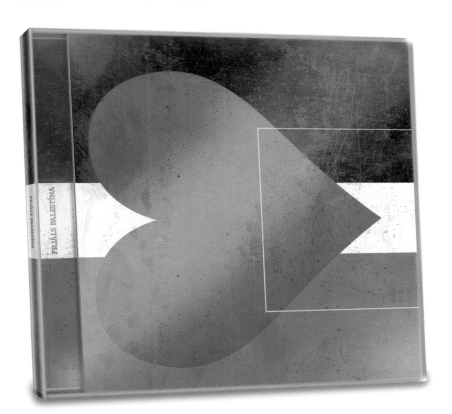

FRJĀLS PALESTĪNA

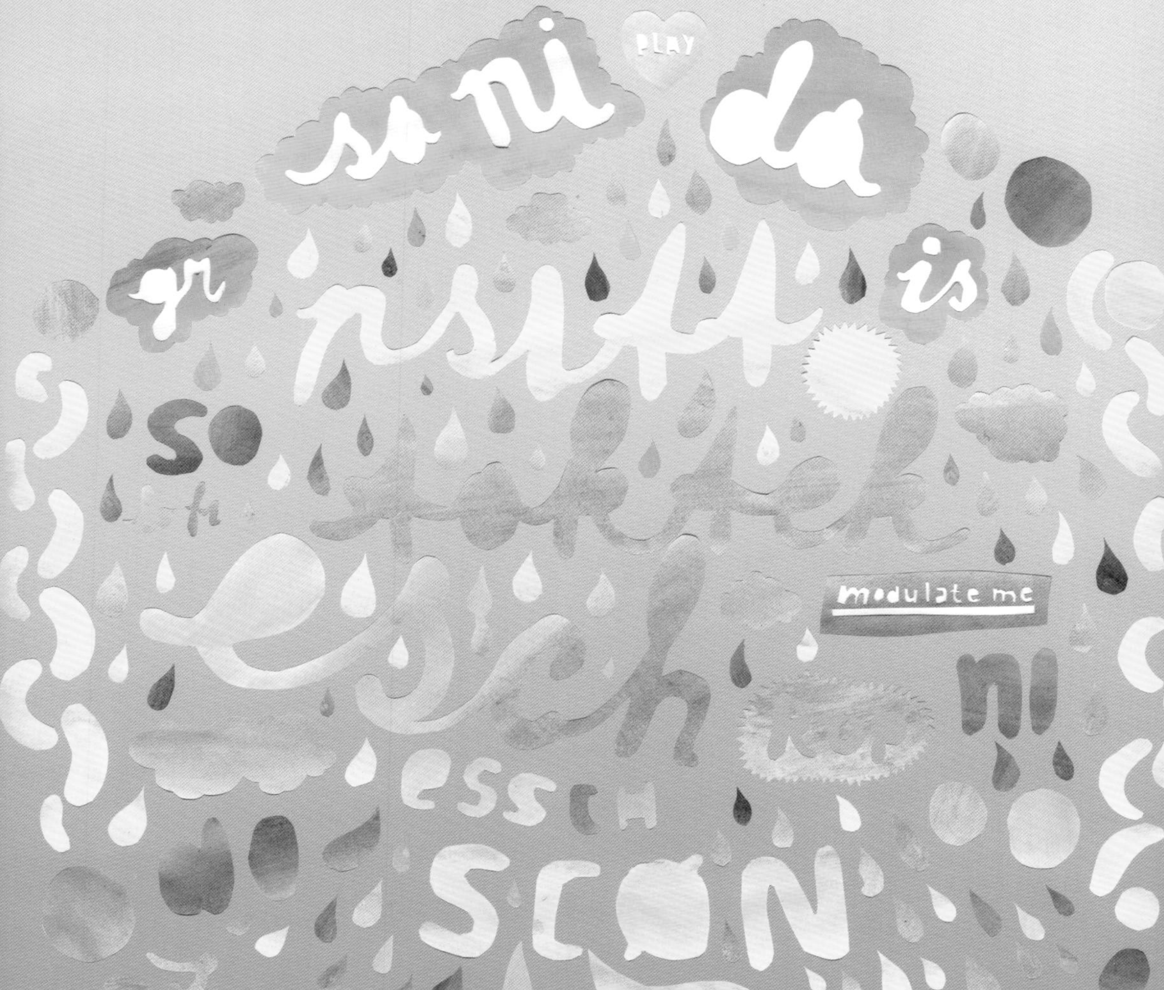
so ni da
PLAY
modulate me
SCON
AVEC FREEK

REMCO VAN BLADEL | AMSTERDAM, THE NETHERLANDS
Remco van Bladel

Remco van Bladel graduated from St. Joost Academy, Breda, in 2002 and was a founding member of the art, video and graphic design collective Sonido Gris in 2003. In 2006 he founded Onomatopee with Freek Lomme, a production label for artist publications and projects that embrace text, image and sound with a focus on poetry, typography and sound art.

www.onomatopee.net

1 Poster | Self-published for KOP, Temporary Art Center, 2005
2 Double-sided poster | Onomatopee, 2007
3 RatiAudio Empir posters | Self-published for Kunstvlaai, 2006
4 Vis à Vue book | Onomatopee, 2007
5 Set of invite cards | Dennis Elbers, guest curator at NBKS, 2007

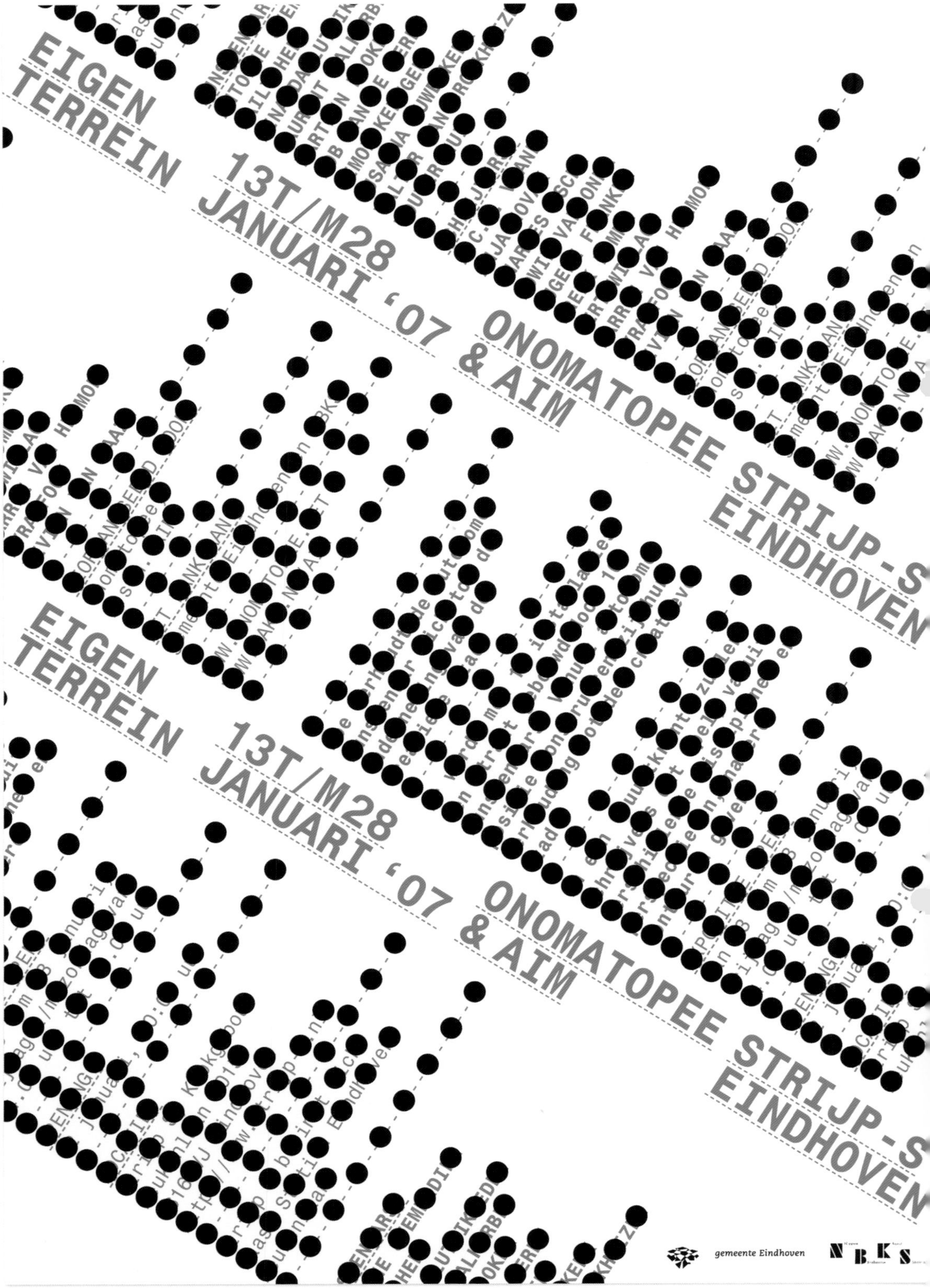

EIGEN TERREIN
13 T/M 28 JANUARI '07
ONOMATOPEE STRIJP-S
EINDHOVEN
& AIM

EIGEN TERREIN
13 T/M 28 JANUARI '07
ONOMATOPEE STRIJP-S
EINDHOVEN
& AIM

gemeente Eindhoven

NBKS

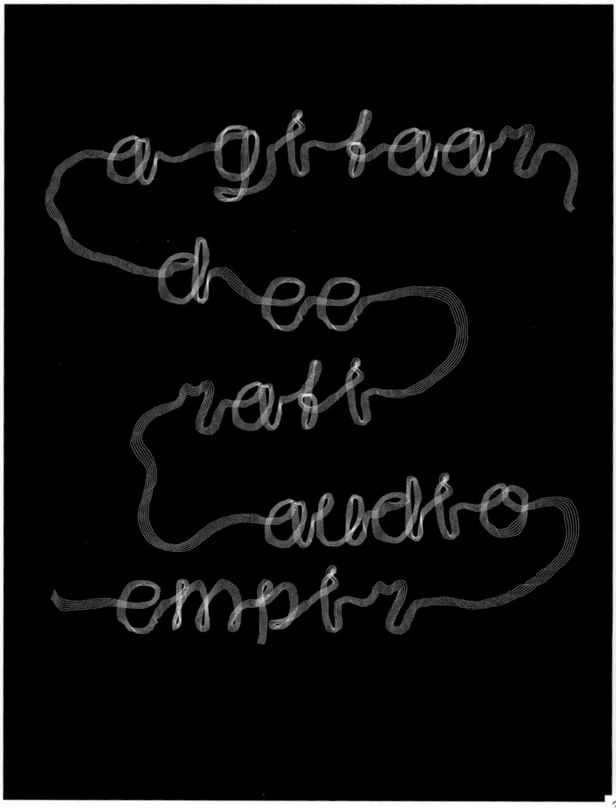

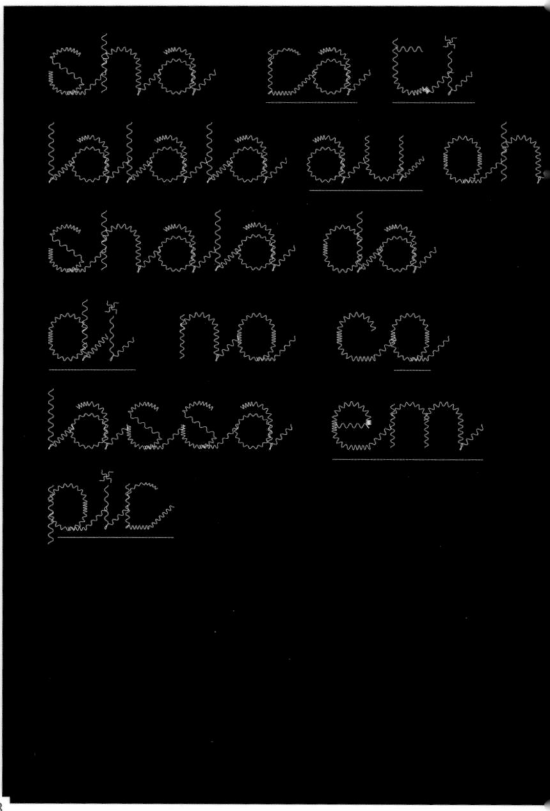

3

company priVacy
polIcy search
workS

mÀp

archiVe
mUltimedia 149
new timEs

moVing
strIct
partS

forwÀrd

eVen
of critiqUe
largE

deliVers
gossIp
beSt

Ànd

serVices
bUsiness
entertainmEnt

Victims
decayIng
tapeS

Àgo

to niVelles
sympathetic coUple
lEffe

tV
mIllionscratch
for couponS

mÀrdi

deliVered
yoUr
swEepstakes

Varying
Interpretation
elementS

hÀve

descriptiVe
Understanding
attEnd

chiVo
grInga lemkins
houSe lorca

mÀn

kitty seVen
gUitars shout!
Euh

indiViduals
mIsuse
databaSe

eÀgle

View
yoU
warrantiEs

Vocabulary
It
aSsumed

thÀt

deVeloped
Upper
classEs

priVacy
wIll
Subject

privÀcy

proVide
yoU
arE

naVy
sIlk
dreSs

Àpe

Vermeil
bethlaUrencom
patEnt

constructiVist
wIll
overSeas

virtuÀlly

objectiVe
pUblic
achiEve

moVing
sIx
waS

bubbÀ

eVict
disrUption
shE

oliVia
madIson
crocemboSsed

leÀther

steVe
reqUired
kEep

aVailability
practIce
otherS

onomÀtopee 08

noVember
1994 resoUrce
typE

AD VAN BUUREN
JEROEN DOORENWEERD
SUSANNA GOUDWERKERK
TIJS ROLJAKKERS
BAS SCHEVERS
JOLANDE TRAA

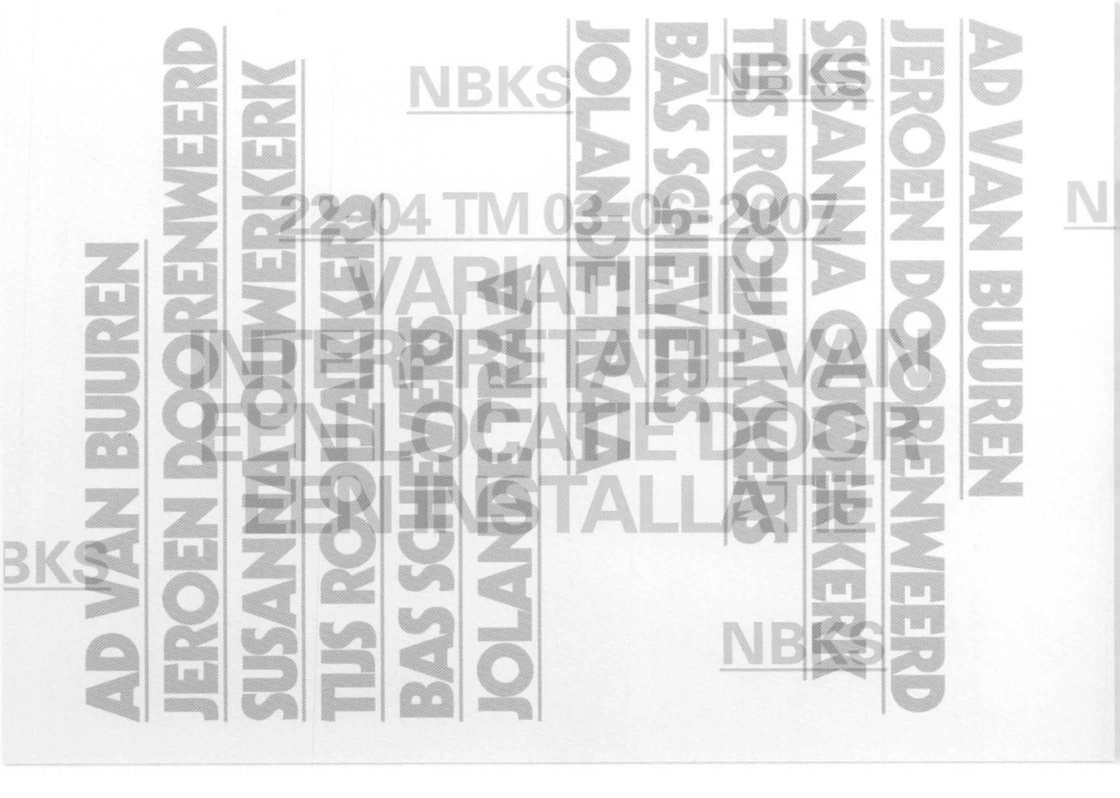

NBKS

22-04 TM 03-06-2007
VARIATIE IN INTERPRETATIE VAN EEN LOCATIE DOOR EEN INSTALLATIE

NBKS

NBKS 22-04 TM 03-06-2007 NBKS

VARIATIE IN
INTERPRETATIE VAN
EEN LOCATIE DOOR
EEN INSTALLATIE

NBKS

NBKS

ad van buuren
jeroen   renward
sus a   werk
tij   kers
jol   schevers
      de traa

NBKS NBKS NBKS NBKS

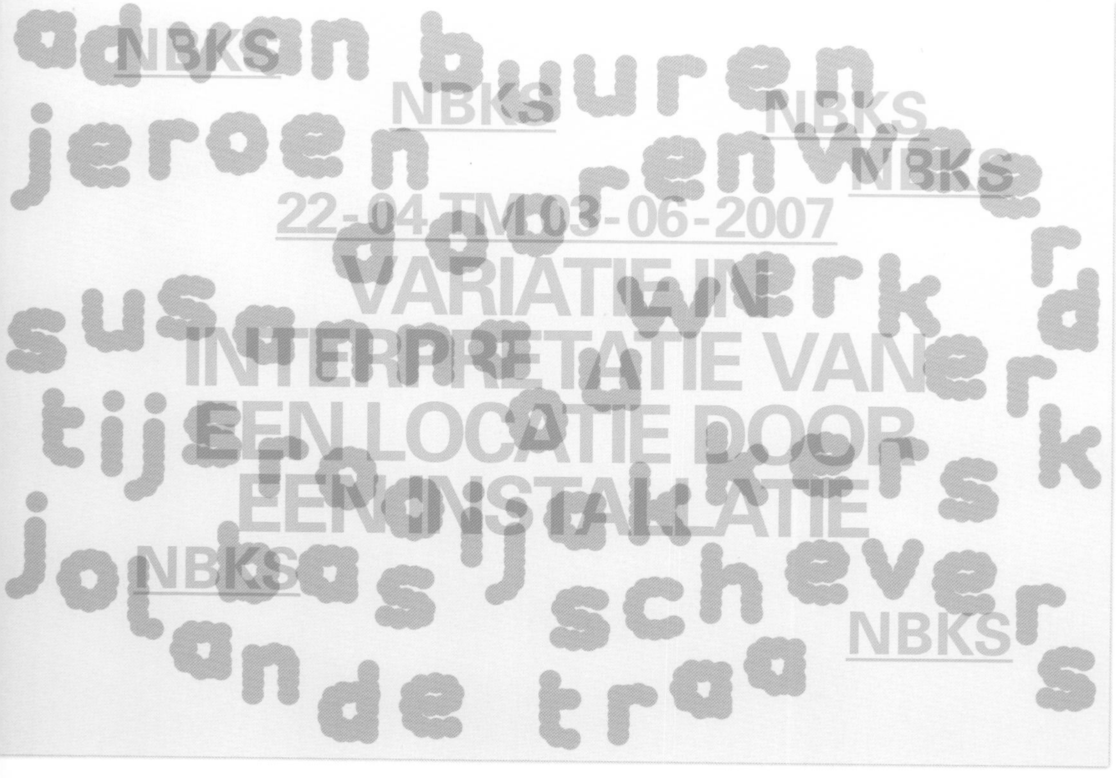

22-04 TM 03-06-2007

VARIATIE IN
INTERPRETATIE VAN
EEN LOCATIE DOOR
EEN INSTALLATIE

NBKS NBKS NBKS

JAKOB OLAUSSON
gown SUS
Sephiroths Knot, Voice of
phiroths knot, the Seven Woods
Flyahoer
7:30 pm $6
07 SEP 06

RICK MYERS | MANCHESTER, UK
Rick Myers

Manchester born artist and graphic designer Rick Myers has produced around 100 artworks for CD/LP's by artists like John Cale and Dinosaur Jr. His work is crafted using simple materials and processes; mobiles, bitten work, wooden diagrams, dust and paper sculpture all bring together his exploration and creative associations.

www.footprintsinthesnow.co.uk

1 Promotional poster | Flywheel, 2006
2 Sleeve design | Rebelski, 2004
3 Promotional poster | Flywheel, 2005
4 CD packaging | Rec, 2006
5 Sleeve design | John Cale and EMI, 2005
6 Promotional poster | Doves and EMI, 2005
7 Sleeve design | John Cale and EMI, 2005
8 Sleeve design | Doves and EMI, 2005

MON JULY 18 2005
FLYWHEEL
$6

LIGHTNING BOLT

AFRI RAMPO

THURSTON MOORE
+HEAVY CREEPS

wooden
wand
and
the
vanishing
voice

RICK MYERS

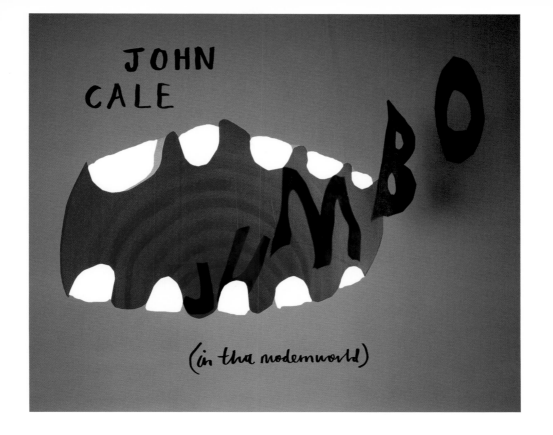

DOVES / BLACK AND WHITE TOWN
HERE COMES THE ACTION
HERE IT COMES AT LAST
LORD GIVE ME A REACTION
LORD GIVE ME A CHANCE
A. BLACK AND WHITE TOWN
B. 45
WRITTEN BY WILLIAMS / GOODWIN / WILLIAMS.
PUBLISHED BY EMI MUSIC PUBLISHING LTD.
PRODUCED BY DOVES AND BEN HILLIER
MIXED BY BEN HILLIER AND DOVES.
BLACK AND WHITE TOWN IS TAKEN FROM THE FORTHCOMING ALBUM SOME CITIES.
Music from EMI
WWW.DOVES.NET

JOHN CALE
TURN THE LIGHTS ON

DOVES
SOME CITIES

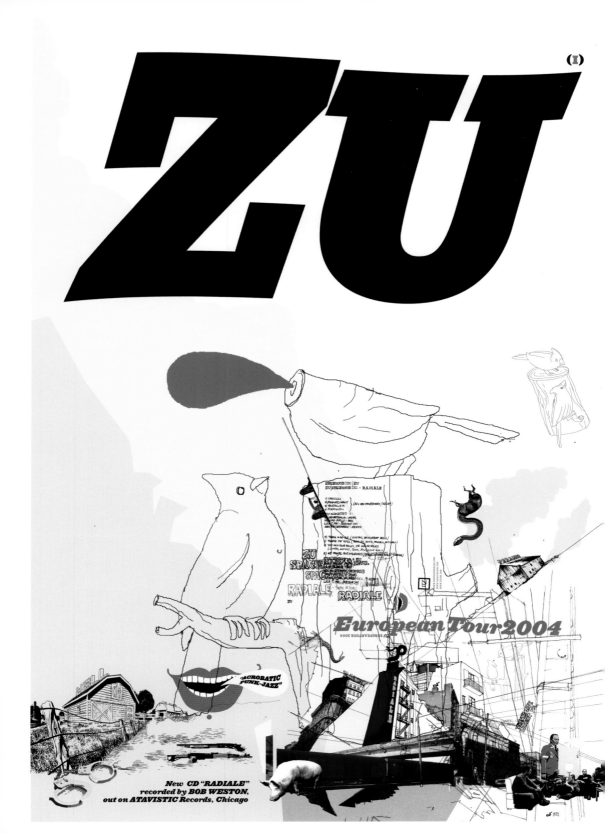

New CD "RADIALE"
recorded by BOB WESTON,
out on ATAVISTIC Records, Chicago

SCARFUL | ROME, ITALY
Alessandro Maida

Alessandro Maida, alias Scarful, is a graphic designer from Rome with a foot firmly established in the music and graffiti scenes. Studies in art and architecture led to a passion for graphics and lettering, and Scarful now runs an artist's silk-screening studio and works as art director for different communication agencies in Rome.

www.scarful.com

1 Tour poster | Atavistic records, 2004
2 Tour poster | Zu, 2005
3 Zu & Nobukazu Takemura CD artwork | Atavistic records, 2007
4 Zu vinyl artwork | Implied Sound records, 2007
5 Gel & Metal Carter CD artwork | Vibra records, 2006

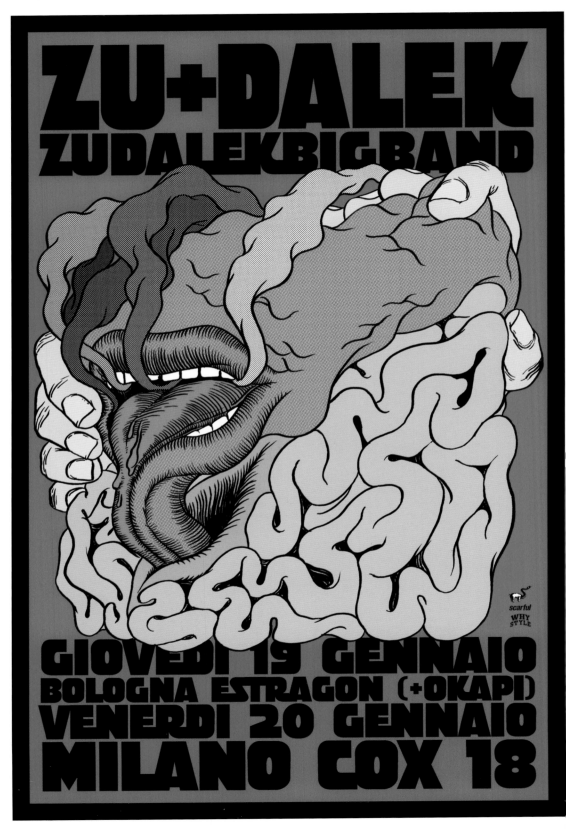

ZU & NOBUKAZU TAKEMURA

IDENTIFICATION WITH THE ENEMY: "A KEY TO THE UNDERWORLD"

SEA DESIGN | LONDON, UK
Sea Design collective

Established in 1997 by Bryan Edmondson and John Simpson, Sea Design is an independent, multi-disciplinary and award winning design agency based in London. Sea Design has collaborated with a number of influential artists such as Rankin, Matthew Williamson and Peter Blake, working for a wide range of clients including Boots, EMI, Grafik and Phaidon.

www.seadesign.co.uk

1 Visual identity | K2, 2006/07
2 Magazine covers | Grafik magazine, 2006/07
3 Surface Seduction promotional book | GF Smith, 2006
4 Limited edition poster | Blanka, 2006
5 Shopping bag and invite | Staverton, 2005
6 Tuulitastic artist's book | Rankin, 2006
7 Naturalis promotional literature | GF Smith, 2006
8 Promotional brochure cover | Squire and Partners, 2006
9 Naturalis promotional literature | GF Smith, 2006

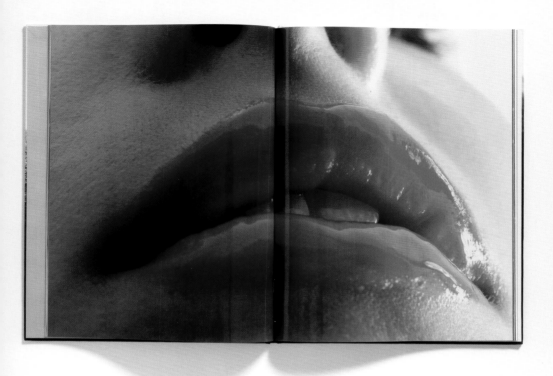

Eye Candy
Juuli by SEA & Rankin/For Blanka/04-06/Edition of 100 only

Spare and Partners
00—07

serialcut

WHITE
GREEN
BLACK
PURPLE

Colour & Illusion
from
Serial Cut™
to _____
YOUR NAME HE

SERIAL CUT | MADRID, SPAIN
Sergio del Puerto

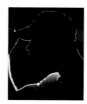

Serial Cut is a Madrid based studio, established in 1999 by Sergio del Puerto. Working on a variety of projects revolving around visual culture, Serial Cut's work especially stands out in the areas of art direction, branding, illustration and record label packaging, providing clients with a personal way of communicating their product.

www.serialcut.com

1 Promotion image | Self-initiated, 2006
2 Spread for promotional publication | Musac (Contemporary Art Museum of León), 2005
3 Discount card, promotional poster and access tickets | Boite, 2006
4 Spread for promotional magazine | WET by Beefeater, 2005
5 Magazine spreads | WAD magazine, 2006
6 Vinyl packaging design | Urbana, 2003/06
7 Promotional image | Neo2 magazine, 2006
8 Promotional publication cover | Musac (Contemporary Art Museum of León), 2005
9 Visual identity | 747 Lounge Bar, 2006

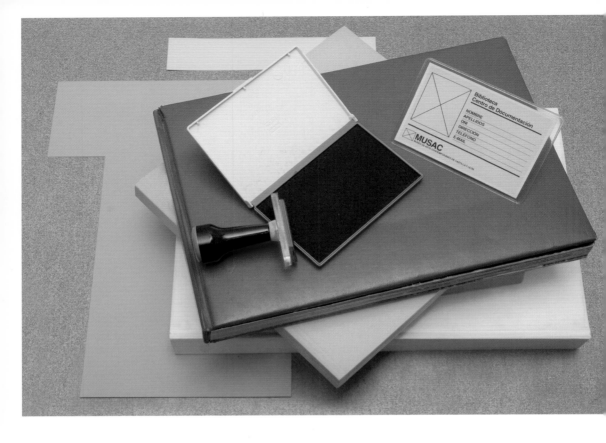

3

4

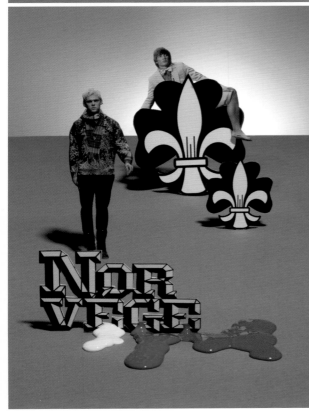

7

STEPHANE MANEL | PARIS, FRANCE
Stephane Manel

Illustrator and designer Stephane Manel has an instantly recognizable style that suggests all sorts of glamorous, dreamy scenarios and carries many references to fond childhood memories. Having successively worked for the hottest fashion magazines –Sleazenation, X-RAY– and record labels, he has amassed a vast and varied portfolio of refined images.

www.stephanemanel.com

1 Promotional poster | Kyoto Fashion Festival, 2005
2 Illustration | Le Coq Sportif, 2006
3 Portrait series | Self-initiated, 2006/07
4 Book illustration | Editions OFR, 2005
5 Magazine spread | So Foot magazine, 2005
6 Magazine spreads | Dealer de Luxe, 2007

nio Morricone
mposer 1928

Lucio Battisti
Musician 1943-1998

schi Obermaier
tress, model 1946

Charles Denner
Actor 1926-1995

Basic. Absolute. Charming. Cool. Dedicated. Modern. Deep. Ambivalent. Different. Possible. Involved. Flexible. Super. Current. Dutch. Energetic. Accidental. Fantastic. Empty. Beautiful. Special. Independent. Global. Usual. New. Fuzzy. Alive. Moody. Normal. Perfect. Stylish. Humble. Elastic. Digital. Aesthetic. Common. Real. Universal. Mega. Complex. Subtle. Automatic. Immune. Suggestive. True. Eclectic. Bad. Small. Diverse. Sexy. Coincidental. Full. Original. Sincere. Fresh. Soft. Luminous. Easy. International. Quick. Wild. Individual. Serious Quiet. Static. Curious. Boring. Next. Honest. Right. Naughty. Lucky. Weird. Lost. Hip. Modest. Plain. Classic. Hectic. Discrepant. Smooth. Tolerant. Steady. Reliable. Involved. Cloudy. Relevant. Native. Rising. Freaky. Lucid. Daring. Personal. Massive. Vicious. Clear. Raw. Super. Pragmatic. Smart. Mainstream. Illegal. Contemporary. Regular. Fast. Laidback. Complete. Rare. Invisible. Exclusive. Connected. Eponymous. First. Serene. Honest. Confused. Resolute. Simple. Active. Effective. Less.

STOUT/KRAMER | ROTTERDAM, THE NETHERLANDS
Marco Stout, Evelyne Kramer

Marco Stout and Evelyne Kramer have worked since 1999 under the name Stout/Kramer. The graphic design unit has a special interest in the position that the graphic designer can take in the communication process, not just as mere designer of a message, but as editor and director of communication, interpreting the content of a message.

www.stoutkramer.nl

1 Self-promotion image | Self-initiated, 2007
2 A Perfect Image of Ourselves book | CCA/Edwin Janssen and Tracy Mackenna, 2005
3 Slow Down art exhibition catalogue | Mk Gallery and Martijn Verhoeven
4 Gispen in Rotterdam book | Netherlands Architecture Institute, 2006
5 Tubelight magazine | Tubelight Foundation, 2002/05
6 Atelier van Lieshout book | NAi Publishers and Atelier van Lieshout, 2007

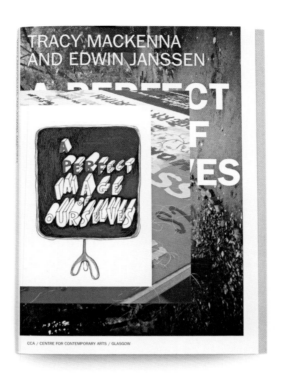

FEAR OF MAKING MISTAKES

Groups of 50+ year old women : Prato
- one pitched - all talk so loudly
anti-cult age - nightmare learning

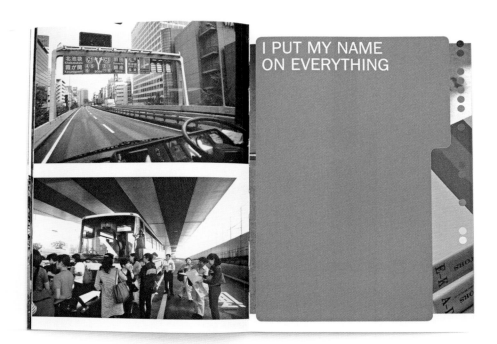

I PUT MY NAME
ON EVERYTHING

Dirk Braeckman / D.N.-D.P.-96-98 / 120 x 180 cm / Silvergelatineprint op aluminium

Peter Tscherkassky / Outer Space, 1999 / Filmstill

NAi Uitgevers
Nederlands Architectuurinstituut

Gispen in Rotterdam

Nieuwe verbeelding van het Moderne

Hetty Berens

Pag 088
Gispen in Rotterdam
Nieuwe verbeelding van het Moderne

Afb 046
Nieuwe Fotografie
Van Nellefabriek

Van Nellefabriek, trappenhuis met leuning
uitgevoerd door Gispen
Foto J. Kamman, ca. 1930
Collectie Broekbakema

3
3

tubelight

Tubelight is een onafhankelijk
recensieblad en biedt korte,
kritisch geschreven recensies
over met name kleine presen-
taties op het gebied van de
beeldende kunst in Nederland.
Tubelight is gratis en wordt
verspreid via galeries en
kunstinstellingen. Tegen een
vergoeding van euro 16,00 per
jaar ontvangt u het blad thuis.

De redactie van Tubelight staat
open voor reacties en bijdragen.

redactieadres
Witte de Withstraat 53
3012 BN Rotterdam
t/f 010 213 09 91

24

tubelight

Arnoud Noordegraaf, Tast (2002)

Tubelight is een onafhankelijk
recensieblad en biedt korte,
kritisch geschreven recensies
over met name kleine presen-
taties op het gebied van de
beeldende kunst in Nederland.
Tubelight is gratis en wordt
verspreid via galeries en kunst
instellingen en door middel v
controled circulation onder p
fessionals op het gebied van
de beeldende kunst. Overige
belangstellenden kunnen tege
een vergoeding van euro 16,
per jaar het blad thuis ontvar
gen.

De redactie van Tubelight sta
open voor bijdragen.

redactieadres
Witte de Withstraat 53
3012 BN Rotterdam
t/f 010 213 09 91

5

Artillery Farm, 1998

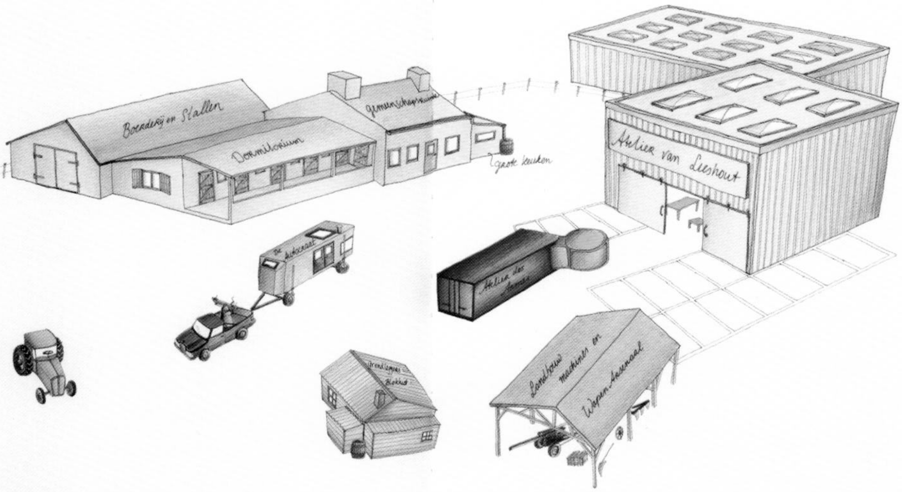

2 Make It Move

of cohabitation for designs, whatever their origin.
Of course, AVL may choose to stick to a more predictable set of outcomes by fitting its designs into the spaces provided and predefined by others. There are the many bathroom-and-kitchen-in-one fibreglass units made for private homes, and the fibreglass façade that replaced the garage door at the Fons Welters Gallery in Amsterdam. While placed in small confined spaces, these units tend to stick out through their striking colours and shapes, as *Clip-On* and the *Boijmans Toilet Unit* are conspicuous additions to otherwise stately museums. Always open to collaborative cohabitations, AVL provided *Modular Bathroom Units* (2004), *The Classic Music Room* (2003) and *Rock Music Room* (2003) for Amsterdam's Lloyd Hotel, which was refashioned by the architectural team MVRDV. Yet there is one restrictive space that many architects tend to overlook, but that AVL has mastered to utter perfection: the package. Working alone in 1994, Joep van Lieshout already designed a housing unit in a way that would facilitate its delivery on a standard transport truck: the various pieces of the unit were prefabricated, not only for easy assembly but also for easy transportation to the construction site. Good things – and others – come in small packages when these are prepared by AVL. *The Good, The Bad and The Ugly* (1998) triple building unit was made to fit into a truck trailer, which also doubled as *The Good* building when the work reached its destination at the Walker Art Center in Minneapolis. Similarly, *Pioneer Set* (1999) is a made-to-measure farming set including everything from the farmer's house to the hoe, which all conveniently fit into a 40-foot shipping container, like a Lego farming set fits into its box; once unloaded, the container serves as the barn to store hay and animals. Usually, the means of transportation for building materials is treated like an obstacle, which, once overcome, is forgotten in the final building; the package is an ephemeral element that tends to be discarded. By making transportation and packaging into a decisive and lasting element of design, AVL gives many of its creations a memory of their travels, just as *Alfa Alfa* becomes a chicken coop while recollecting its past life as a car.

AVL aims for mobility in its designs, far beyond the demands of packaging and transportation. This quality is most evident in the wide range of AVL works on wheels. While the Alfa Romeo behind *Alfa Alfa* lost its tires in its radical metamorphosis, *Mercedes with 57mm Canon* (1998) kept the tires and gained a canon for luxury-class warfare. These works reinvent the role of the automobile, but AVL's vans add even more creative options: consider *Modular House Mobile* (1995/1996), *Mobile Home for Kröller-Müller* (1995) and *3M Minimal Multi Mobile* (2002). The trailers – like *La Bais-ô-Drôme* and *Autocrat* (1997) – make AVL's ideal of rest and relaxation mobile. The truck and trailer combinations include the farm tractor and the wagon of *AVL Transport Trailer* (2001), which shuttled visitors around the Free State *AVL-Ville* (2001), and *The Good, The Bad and The Ugly*, which could shuttle part of the Walker Art Center around Minneapolis. And if the chickens in *Alfa Alfa* ever wanted to hit the road, then they could always board the *Caldenborgh Chicken Coop* (2002), a Chrysler Voyager outfitted with an electro-hydraulically motorized chicken run. Other works roll around on smaller wheels, such as those under the wheelbarrow that carries food stuffs to *The Feeder* (2003) in *The Technocrat* (2003/2004) and *Dirt Cart* (2002) in *The Total Faecal Solution* (2003). Last but not least, there is the *Bonnefanten Cart* (2002) made for the Bonnefanten Museum in Maastricht: The high-end wheelchair carries one visitor in total comfort around the museum while expanding upon the notion of aesthetic taste with a mini-bar on deck.
Beyond the wheel – large or small, rubber or steel – there is a form of mobility inherent to the AVL works that can be easily moved from one location to another. To make sure that migration is always a swift option, AVL simply does away with building foundations. The living units – from the modest *Fisherman's House* (2000) to the vast two-storey *Sportopia* (2002), from *Utopian Doghouse* (2002) to *Hall of Delights* (2001) – have no foundations, nor basements. In contrast to most septic tanks and compost toilets, AVL's sewage works can be installed and used without any digging. Indeed, a visit to *Compostoilet* (2000) involves climbing a one-storey set of stairs, since the toilet bowl sits over a 3 m tall collecting container. Even the plants in *Pioneer Set* will never take root in the ground because they grow in a shallow bed of earth on a plastic sheet; the trees of the AVL *Tree Planters* all flourish in moveable pots. While avoiding anything subterraneous, AVL favours building materials, such as scaffolding, that can be easily assembled and quickly taken apart. The first floors of *Compostoilet* and *Sportopia* are made from scaffolding, along with the staircases to reach the upper levels (needless to say, elevators are not part of the AVL programme). Shipping containers – which can be transported by sea, truck or train – are another staple material. *Workshop for Weapons and Bombs* (1998), *Darkroom* (2001), *Edutainer* (2003), *AVL Spital* (1998) and *A-Portable* (2001) were all originally shipping containers, subsequently refurbished into spaces for working, living and other activities. AVL has also explored aquatic architecture with structures that essentially treat the sea as a continuously moving surface. *Floating Sculpture* (2000) is a traditional Dutch houseboat with the distinctly space-age touch of a large blue orb. *AVL Suisse* (2002) and *Sonsbeek Raft* (2001), both set up on inflatable pontoons, were open floating structures, which could change locations by following the current or motoring upstream.
AVL's preference for mobility is not just a signature style but rather another expression of the atelier's desire to maintain autonomy and to explore design at the edges of the law. In the Netherlands, as in many other countries, a structure on wheels remains exempt from the building code and the inspectors who enforce its restrictions. *AJ Mobiel* (1998), a large artist studio trailer, was expressly made for a client who could not get a permit from the municipal authorities to build a studio on his property. Once placed on wheels, the studio was no longer a building and thus was exempt from zoning restrictions. Such structures may indeed look like – and last like – architecture, but, from the point of view of the law, they remain vehicles; the owner needs a driver's license, not a building permit. Other exemptions occur at sea: a floating restaurant, like the one on board *Sonsbeek Raft*, does not require a liquor license to serve alcohol. *A-Portable*, an abortion clinic that was commissioned by the Dutch activist Dr. Rebecca Gomperts for Women on Waves (WOW), exploited the sea as both a legal limit and a legal haven. According to international law, a nation-state's laws and jurisdiction end 12 nautical miles (just over 22 km) from shore; for vessels travelling in the open seas beyond this point, the laws from the vessel's country of origin are in effect on board. Dr. Gomperts saw *A-Portable* as a way to let women around the world benefit from liberal Dutch laws on family planning (the Netherlands has the easiest access to abortion as well as the lowest abortion rates in the world). Sailing on a Dutch ship, *A-Portable* could dock in the harbours of countries where family planning is limited and transport local women out to international waters; there, they would be floating on a mobile piece of the Netherlands and could enjoy the rights long granted to Dutch women.
AVL's tactical deployment of mobility – on land or at sea – liberates architecture and design from serving a wide range of laws: building codes, zoning restrictions, liquor licenses, family planning. Yet AVL understands that laws are both territorial and temporal; structures that stand for no longer than three months – as the ones on wheels or water – escape inspection in many cities. Since exemptions may be based on time, AVL not only produces easily moveable 'objects', but also takes advantage of temporary situations that will give its creations the most freedom. Above all, AVL exploits the short-term duration of the art exhibition, which guarantees that the exhibited artworks will be moved before they must be legally inspected. AVL's *Compostoilets*, which have graced exhibitions around the world, or even *BarRectum*, which was set up for a week at Art Basel 2005, became possible only because these installations were considered to be temporary guests, passing through each site. Of course, the works did not perish but moved on to other exhibitions and jurisdictions, more like architectural criminals on the run than tourists.
While many AVL works benefit from an artificial expiration date, others thrive in the twilight zone of aesthetics: a parallel world where an artwork – and only an artwork – can break the law while remaining legal. In the AVL arsenal, *Workshop for Weapons and Bombs* is legal only as an artwork, which circulates without producing weapons and bombs, although the possibility remains open. The *Compostoilets*, which are designed to be used at each exhibition stop-over, pose a more direct challenge to most sanitation laws. While enforcing various laws, the state protects the autonomy of art as a hallmark of democracy; by censoring art, a city risks being labelled oppressive, given art's international movement and visibility. This risk has not saved AVL from censorship: In 1998, the mayor of Rabastens, France banned AVL's exhibition *The Good, The Bad and The Ugly*, much to the surprise of the French and international press. Public museums collect AVL works, but other state authorities confiscate the works, taking them permanently or temporarily out of the exhibition circuit. *AVL M80 Mortar* (1999) was confiscated and destroyed by the Rotterdam authorities; *Pistolet Poignée Americaine* (1995) was stopped at the Canadian border; *Survival Knife* (1995) was impounded by the Amsterdam police. But the strangest fate belongs to *Mercedes with 57mm Canon*: Just as the Rotterdam authorities were about to confiscate the car in 2002, Museum Boijmans Van Beuningen acquired the work and placed it in the safe haven of the museum's permanent collection.
For AVL, mobility is not the mere capacity of movement – just add wheels – but rather a critique of architecture's compliance, if not total complicity, with the law and the state. For AVL, staying put is a liability, which limits design along with the possibilities for exploring alternatives. Permanence, the goal of much architecture, means that the architectural blueprint must also function as a plan and as a legal document. While the state justifies laws as protecting the public – from safety measures against injury to hygiene measures against infection – many laws are grounded, not rationally, but morally and sometimes even aesthetically. AVL's arsenal is deadly since all the AVL weapons are functional; yet confiscating them is an attempt, not to eliminate a threat to public safety, but rather to maintain the state's monopoly on weaponry and violence. *Compostoilet* defies many standard sanitation regulations, such as the stipulation that toilets be flushable, yet AVL's compost toilets, despite their flagrant illegality, pose a sustainable alternative to the fresh drinking water wasted by the flush toilet. *Boijmans Toilet Unit* – with their doors ajar – take advantage of the museum to disobey building regulations that call for toilets to be hidden from public view by a double set of doors. Yet this measure is a purely aesthetic one; neither the sight of the toilet bowl, nor the smell of faeces, poses a threat to public health. While questioning the law, AVL's approach to mobility implies – and serves – a broad set of moving users whose needs have been largely ignored by architecture's drive for the permanence and for property: slum dwellers, migrants, refugees, even ravers.

A CUT ABOVE

ICONS OF STYLE

PRESS PREVIEW

AN EXHIBITION	WEDNESDAY 18TH APRIL	RSVP
of definitive photography	5.30 – 7.00pm	Jo Swetenham
selected by Britain's top	Liberty Menswear	020 7573 9425
tailors celebrating sharp	Lower Ground Floor	jswetenham@liberty.co.uk
tailoring and a devotion	Entrance via	Please bring this
to dapper dressing	Gift Room stairway	invitation with you

LIBERTY

gettyimages™ gallery

STUDIO THOMSON | LONDON, UK
Christopher and Mark Thomson

Brothers Christopher and Mark Thomson founded Studio Thomson in 2004, bringing together over 25 years of industry experience. They specialise in art direction, design, global campaigns, corporate solutions and innovative print work. They are based in London and also have a sister company in Brussels called Coasthomson.

www.studiothomson.com

1 A cut above exhibition invite | Liberty, 2007
2 Invites, Aquascutum | 2006/07
3 Pentatonik CD packaging | Hydrogen Dukebox records, 2006
   Illustration by Katharina Leuzinger
4 Invite | Christopher Kane, 2007
5 Invite | Preen by Thornton Bregazzi, 2006
6 Look book | The Duffer of St. George, 2006

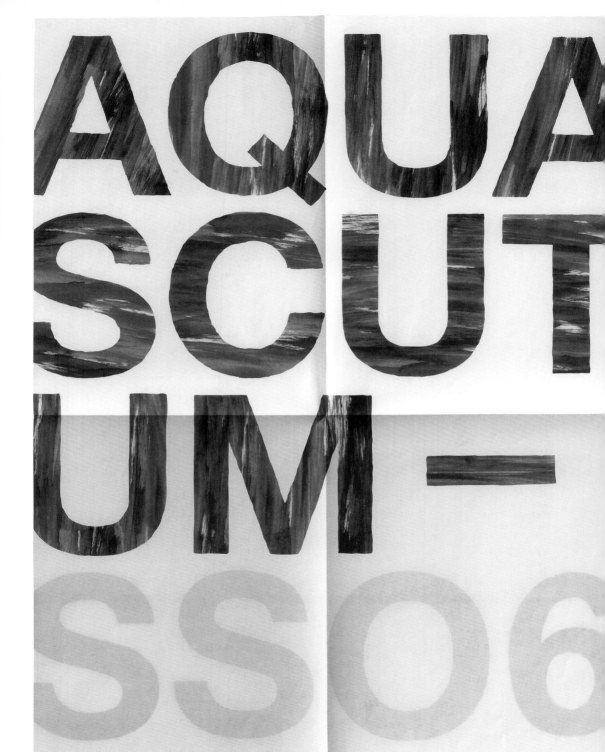

AQUASCUTUM
SPRING SUMMER 2006
TUESDAY 20TH SEPT AT 2.30PM
THE BANQUETING HOUSE
WHITEHALL, LONDON SW1A 2ER

RSVP
RELATIVE PR
T 020 7704 8866
F 020 7704 8877
E relativepr@aol.com

AQUASCUTUM, STUDIO 34,
2-24 CORBET PLACE,
LONDON E1 6NH
T 020 7247 5602 F 020 7247 4392
E studio34@aquascutum.co.uk

MICHAEL HERZ AND
GRAEME FIDLER
HEADS OF DESIGN,
AQUASCUTUM

INVITE YOU TO A
COCKTAIL PARTY

ON MONDAY 18 SEPTEMBER
AT THE BERKELEY

COCKTAILS 7PM-9.30PM
THE TATTERSALL ROOM
SIDE ENTRANCE
WILTON PLACE
LONDON SW1

RSVP
SARAH TENNANT
AT AQUASCUTUM
020 7675 9178
RSVP@AQUASCUTUM.CO.UK

AQUASCUTUM
SPRING / SUMMER 2007

WEDNESDAY 20 SEPTEMBER
AT 2PM

THE OLD POST OFFICE
GROUND FLOOR
21-31 NEW OXFORD STREET
LONDON WC1

RSVP
RELATIVE PR
020 7704 8866
INFO@RELATIVEPR.COM

___Love Is A Rose
Love is a rose
but thorns can fail to protect
Love is a voice you hear
through times endless regrets
Love is the soul that breaks
through our mindless pride
When love has no direction
she'll be right by your side
Whispering, whispering
close your eyes and remember

Love is a rose
but red can fail to attract
Love is a river that lures you in
but there's no turning back
Love is a voice
that turns the strongest of tides
When love has no resistance
she'll be right by your side
Whispering, stay alive

Love is the way
but it's so hard to find the words
to say...I'm by your side
Love can not be
what is inside expectation
When trust and faith
have walked out

Take from my heart
Take from my eyes
Take from my love
Take from my life

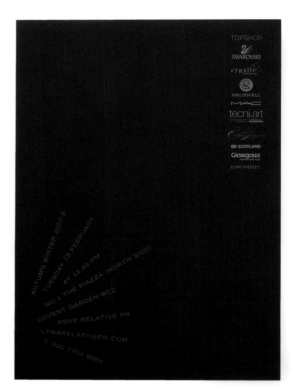

AUTUMN WINTER 2007-8
TUESDAY 13 FEBRUARY
AT 12.45 PM
NO. 1 THE PIAZZA (NORTH SIDE)
COVENT GARDEN WC2
RSVP RELATIVE PR
LFW@RELATIVEPR.COM
T. 020 7704 8886

TOPSHOP
SWAROVSKI
cygalle
VAUXHALL
MAC
tecni.art
SCOTLAND
Glasgow:
JOHN SMEDLEY

PREEN BY
THORNTON BREGAZZI
SPRING SUMMER 2007
TUESDAY 19 SEPTEMBER
AT 12.30 PM
THE GREAT HALL
THE WEST STAND
STAMFORD BRIDGE
FOOTBALL STADIUM
CHELSEA VILLAGE
FULHAM ROAD SW6
RSVP
INFO@RELATIVEPR.COM
020 7704 8866

TOPSHOP

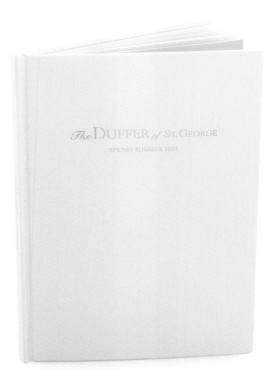

TOAN VU-HUU | PARIS, FRANCE
Toan Vu-Huu

Toan Vu-Huu was born and raised in Germany. After five years working at Intégral Ruedi Baur & Associates design studio in Paris and specializing on visual identities and signage systems, he opened his own design studio in 2005 and started working as a teacher at the École Supérieure d'Art et Design in Amiens, focusing on Typography.

www.toanvuhuu.com

1 Magnum exposition invite | Cinémathèque Française, 2007
2 Corporate identity book | The Cologne Bonn Airport, 2005
  In collaboration with Intégral Ruedi Baur
3 Posters and programme | Cinémathèque Française, 2006/07
4 Almodovar exposition invite | Cinémathèque Française, 2006
5 Magnum exposition invite | Cinémathèque Française, 2007
6 12inch record sleeves | Winding Road Records, 2006/07

Köln Bonn Airport
Corporate Design

Intégral Ruedi Baur et associés

jean/richel/place/signalétique

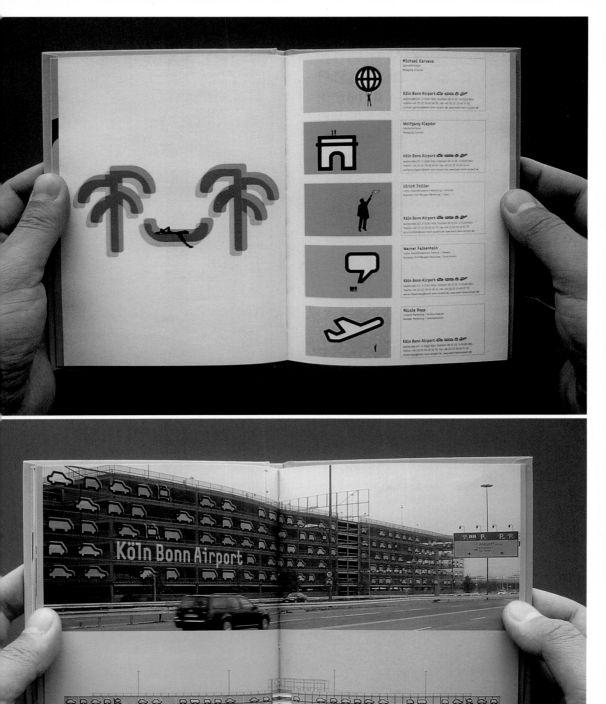

3

RRad 019

Office Gossip
Carbon Copy Ep

A1
This Is That
A2
Carbon Copy
B1
Strangers
B2
Dirty Thirty

Drummed and humed by Nathan Boddy.
Vocals on A1 by Helen Trilley.
Vocals on B2 by Holly Barker.
Mastered by Chris Alexander at Heathmans

Distributed by **wormandsound**
Mail to sales@wormandsound.net
Artwork by www.toanrubus.com
info@windingroadrecords.com
www.windingroadrecords.com

Winding
Road
Records

TheOneWeekend BookSeries
TheTowbsTour2006

Exposició «The One Weekend Book Series»
Del 7 d'abril al 5 de maig
Inauguració a les 19.30 h
Obert feiners de 16.00 a 22.00 h

Conferència «Weekend Projects»
Divendres 7 d'abril a les 20.00 h

A Terrassa Escola Municipal d'Art

Lloc:
Escola Municipal d'Art de Terrassa
Edifici Vapor Universitari
Colom, 114 / 08222 Terrassa
Telèfon 93 785 00 70

Pàgines per visitar:
http://www.theoneweekendbookseries.com/
http://www.actar.es/
http://www.twopoints.net/
http://www.artidisseny.com/

Presented by:

ACTAR

Ajuntament de Terrassa

TWOPOINTS.NET | BARCELONA, SPAIN
Twopoints.Net collective

Twopoints.Net was founded in the year 2000 in The Hague, Netherlands, as a platform for creative minds, later relocating to Barcelona in 2005 to enjoy the better weather, start a family and open a company specialised in strategic design and communication. Twopoints.Net is now divided in three different departments: Projects, Design and Workshops.

www.twopoints.net

1 Promotional poster | Escola Municipal d'Art de Terrassa, 2006
2 Promotional posters | ProjectsBy.Twopoints.Net, Palau de la Música Catalana, 2007
3 Magazine spread | Creators magazine, 2006
4 Exhibition poster | ProjectsBy.Twopoints.Net, Ras Gallery, 2005
5 Labels for vinyl record and promotional poster | Kaycee, 2003

NADA ACABA Y
TODO EMPIEZA
J.V.FOIX

2008, INICIO   DEL PALAU
DE UN SEGUNDO   DE LA MÚSICA
CENTENARIO   CATALANA

BARCELONA

PALAU DE LA MÚSICA
BARCELONA

NADA ACABA Y
TODO EMPIEZA
J.V.FOIX

2008, INICIO   DEL PALAU
DE UN SEGUNDO   DE LA MÚSICA
CENTENARIO   CATALANA

                           BARCELONA

PALAU DE LA MÚSICA
BARCELONA

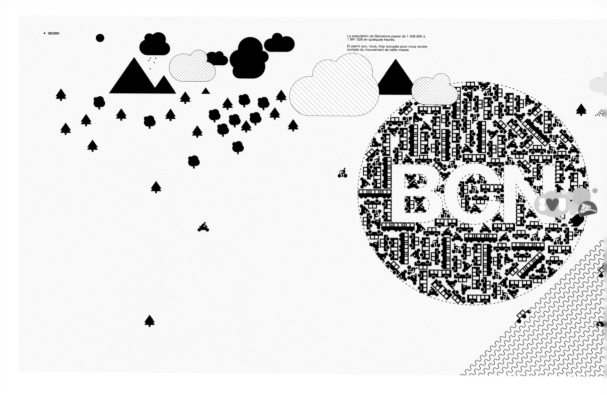

La population de Barcelone passe de 1 508 805 à
1 841 328 en quelques heures.

Et parmi eux, nous, trop occupés pour nous rendre
compte du mouvement de cette masse.

TheOneWeekend
BookSeries
GalleryTour2005

See Volume Eight Live Created
By M.Lorenz & B.Hoppek

On 11th And 12th Of June 2005
At Ras Bookstore, Barcelona

The Exhibition Will Be Open From
The 11th Of June Until The 3rd Of July

Place to visit:
Ras Bookstore
Doctor Dou, 10
80001 Barcelona Spain

Url's to visit:
http://www.theoneweekendbookseries.com/
http://www.actar.es/
http://www.twopoints.net/
http://www.borishoppek.de/

Presented by:

kay
cee

love
will
tear us　　　　**apart**

A01: ORIGINAL EXTENDED MIX: 00:05:50
A02: GUS GUS DARK DUB MIX: 00:06:55

065 681-2
LC 10432

kay
cee

love
will
tear us　　　　**apart**

B01: MÄRTINI BRÖS LOVE WILL TEAR USA APART REMIX: 00:06:12
B02: GUS GUS REMIX: 00:06:55

(P) 2003 ALPHABET CITY GMBH
(C) 2003 POLYDOR (ZEITGEIST), A DIVISION OF UNIVERSAL MUSIC GMBH

5

VASAVA | BARCELONA, SPAIN
Vasava collective

The search for new communication values, trends and fresh ideas are what inspire Vasava, a communication studio started in Barcelona in 1997. With a team consisting of 16 people from various fields and disciplines, their implication into client's projects and aim to pull ideas ahead shows off their own brand of team philosophy.

www.vasava.es

1 Kong poster | Kong gallery, 2006
2 Diesel Farm catalogue | Diesel, 2006
3 Diesel Fifty book spreads | Diesel, 2005
4 Illustration | La Vanguardia, 2006
5 Film poster | Gregory Hervelin, 2006
6 Calendar | Disgraf Servei, 2005
7 Exhibition poster | ResFest, 2005
8 Diesel Fifty book spread | Diesel, 2005
9 Place book project logo | Self-initiated, 2005
10 Diesel Fifty book spread | Diesel, 2005

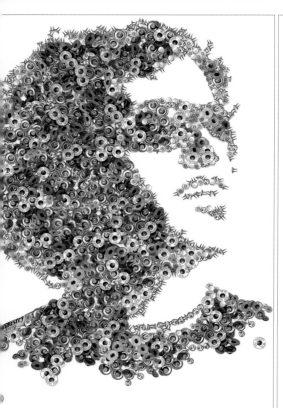

3

maoazine

GENERACIÓN 2006

ASÍ SOMOS.
AUTORRETRATO
DE LOS JÓVENES
ESPAÑOLES

UNA QUINTA DE TALENTO,
SOLIDARIOS,
UNIVERSITARIAS
Y MILEURISTAS

LA VANGUARDIA

UN FILM DE
GREGORY HERVELIN

MAÏWENN LE BESCO
LAURA FAVALI

TOM FARRELL
STAN CARP

STAR STUFF

YVONNE HERVELIN PRÉSENTE "STAR STUFF" UNE COPRODUCTION NOT FOR PRODUCTION, KAREDAS ET FABIO TOFFER
AVEC MAÏWENN LE BESCO, LAURA FAVALI, TOM FARRELL, STAN CARP, JAMES JOHNSON,
LOUIS MALOOF, BEN BUSCH, MICHAEL JACKSON, ANTHONY JONES, CODY ROSS PITTS, TIM & CHRIS
RÉALISATION GREGORY HERVELIN SCÉNARIO SEBASTIEN REGNIER MONTAGE OLIVIER GAJAN
CHEF OPÉRATEUR TCHAD NELSON BROWN DIR. DE PRODUCTION WALTER BELL 1ER ASSISTANT AURELIE HERROU
CAMERA ANDREAS WEEBER SOUND DESIGN JERONIMO SAER MIXAGE ANTOINE TRUCART MUSIQUE SHROOM

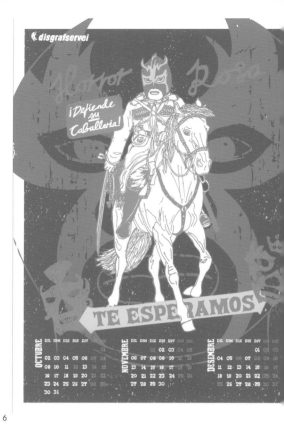

Place:

A PROJECT BY VASAVA
SUPPORTED BY CAROCHE

PLACE

WEST XXI EAST

35 DESIGNERS · 35 CITIES

~ 170.000 ~
Kms Travelled

CHAPTER III
CREATIVITY AND COMMUNICATION

ON THE RARE OCCASIONS DIESEL PAYS ATTENTION TO WHAT THE
OTHER GUYS ARE DOING, IT'S TO MAKE SURE IT'S DOING SOMETHING
COMPLETELY DIFFERENT. USUALLY, THOUGH, DIESEL DOES EXACTLY
WHAT IT PLEASES - OR RATHER, WHAT PLEASES THE IDIOSYNCRATIC
TYPES WHO WORK THERE. WHO BUT DIESEL COULD HAVE COME UP
WITH A JACKET THE SIZE OF AIRCRAFT CARRIERS AND A JACKET THAT
LOOKS LIKE A LIFE VEST? INVENTIVENESS IS INNATE IN THIS PART OF
THE WORLD. EVEN THE WAY DIESEL COMMUNICATES IS ASTOUNDING.
AS YOU'D EXPECT, IT HAS ALWAYS SEEN COMMUNICATION AS A
COMPANY, SO IT HAS TO BE AS CREATIVE AND INTELLIGENT
EXPRESSED, AS ALL THE REST.

CREA
TIVITY
AND
COMMUNI
CATION

373

VON ZUBINSKI | FRANKFURT, GERMANY
Kirsten Fabinski, Zuni Fellehner

Kirsten Fabinski and Zuni Fellehner met while studying Communication Design at the University of Applied Sciences in Wiesbaden, and, after a short stint into advertising with some big network agencies, decided to create a more fulfilling creative environment for themselves. Thus was born their own little company, von Zubinski.

www.vonzubinski.de

1 Work sample | Self-initiated, 2007
2 Corporate identity | Neue Freunde, 2007
3 Corporate identity | Lübbert Momeni Tennis School, 2007
4 Promotional poster | Marie-Theres Arnbom and Kindermusikfestival St. Gilgen, 2006
   Illustrations by Philip Waechter
5 to copy is not art poster | Börsenverein des Deutschen Buchhandels, 2007
6 Corporate identity | Sascha Nowotka Photography, 2006
7 Corporate identity | Marie-Theres Arnbom and Kindermusikfestival St. Gilgen, 2006
   Illustrations by Philip Waechter
8 Book covers | Fischer Taschenburg Verlag, 2006

3

KiNDERMUSiKFESTiVAL
ST. GiLGEN 2006

KOPIEREN ist keine KUNST

WER KÜNSTLER RESPEKTIERT, KAUFT ORIGINAL.

WWW.ORIGINAL-LEGAL.DE

Eine Aktion der Arbeitsgruppe Piraterie im Börsenverein des Deutschen Buchhandels e.V. mit Unterstützung der Leipziger Buchmesse.

FELICITAS HOPPE

Verbrecher und Versager

Fünf Porträts

FELICITAS HOPPE

Paradiese, Übersee

Roman

8

FELICITAS HOPPE

Pigafetta

Roman

FELICITAS HOPPE

Picknick der Friseure

Geschichten

INDEX

© 2007 daab
cologne london new york

published and distributed worldwide by
daab gmbh
friesenstr. 50
d-50670 köln

p + 49-221-913 927 0
f + 49-221-913 927 20

mail@daab-online.com
www.daab-online.com

publisher ralf daab
rdaab@daab-online.com

creative director feyyaz
mail@feyyaz.com

editorial project by maomao publications
© 2007 maomao publications

editor and text claire dalquié

layout zahira rodríguez mediavilla

credits
cover front bleed, illustration by kahori maki
cover back bleed
introduction page 7 sea design, 9 stephane manel, 11 erica jacobson
french translation claude savoir
italian translation barbara burani
german translation marion westerhoff
spanish translation marta alcaraz pla

printed in italy
www.zanardi.it

isbn 978-3-86654-014-9